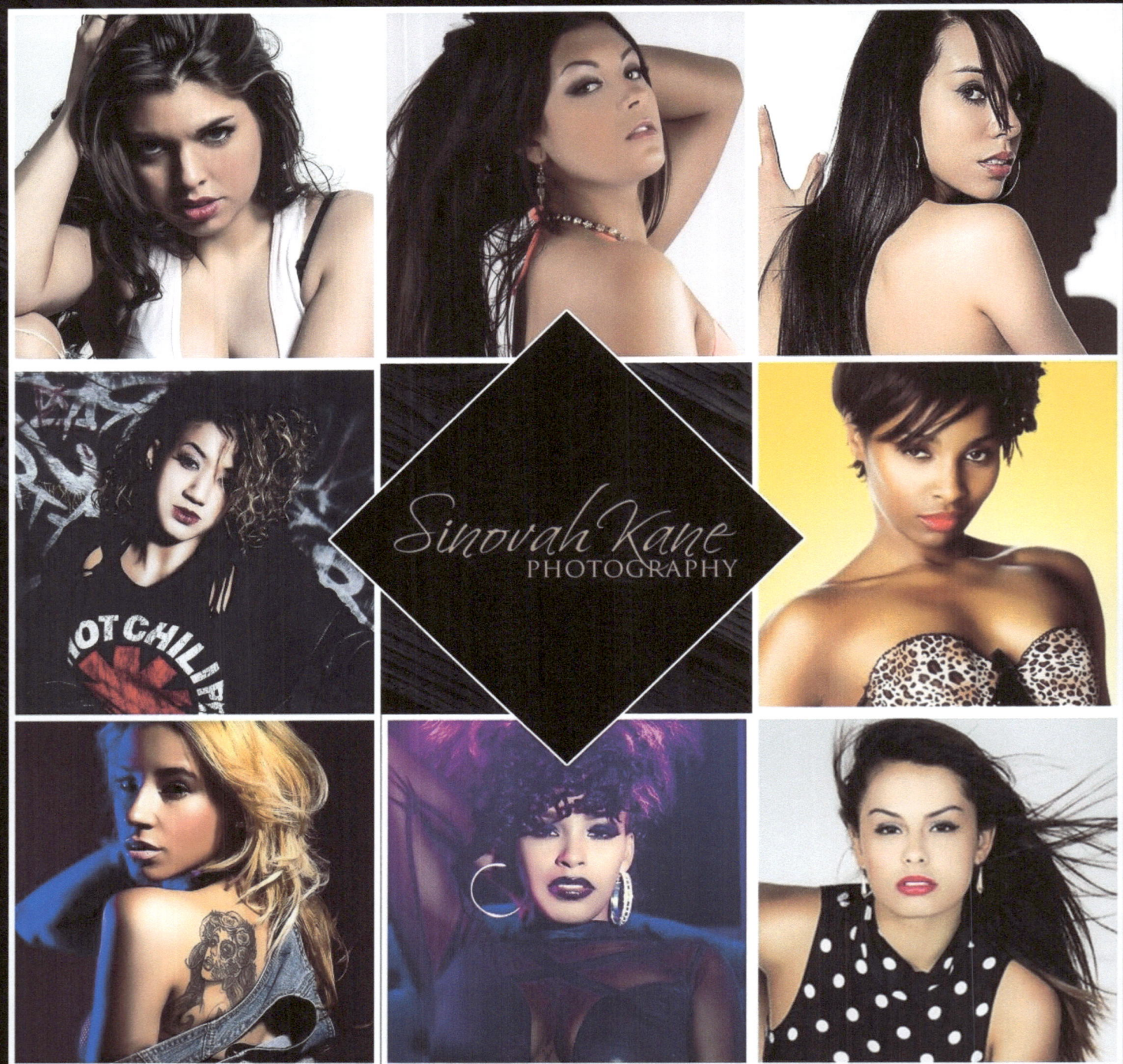

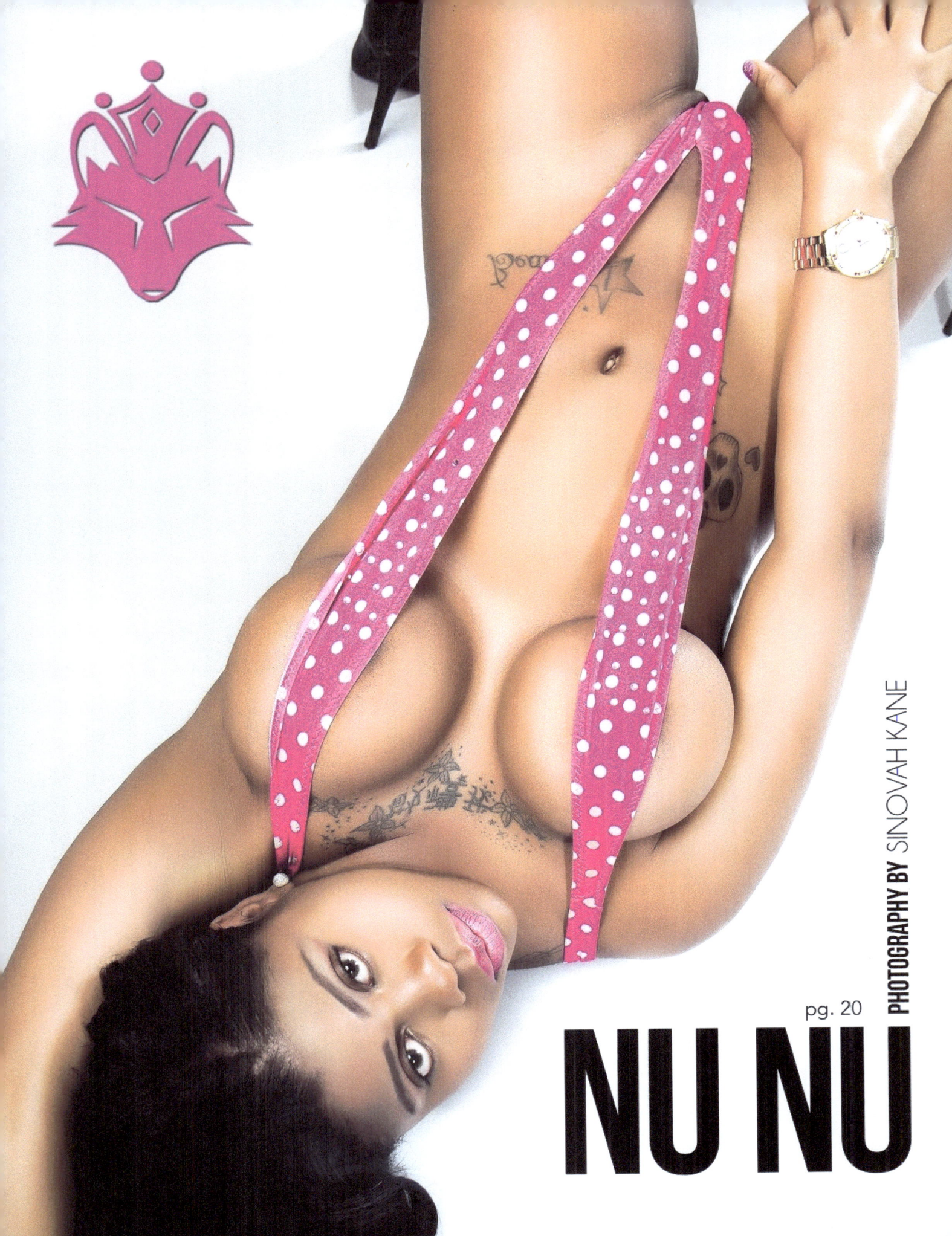

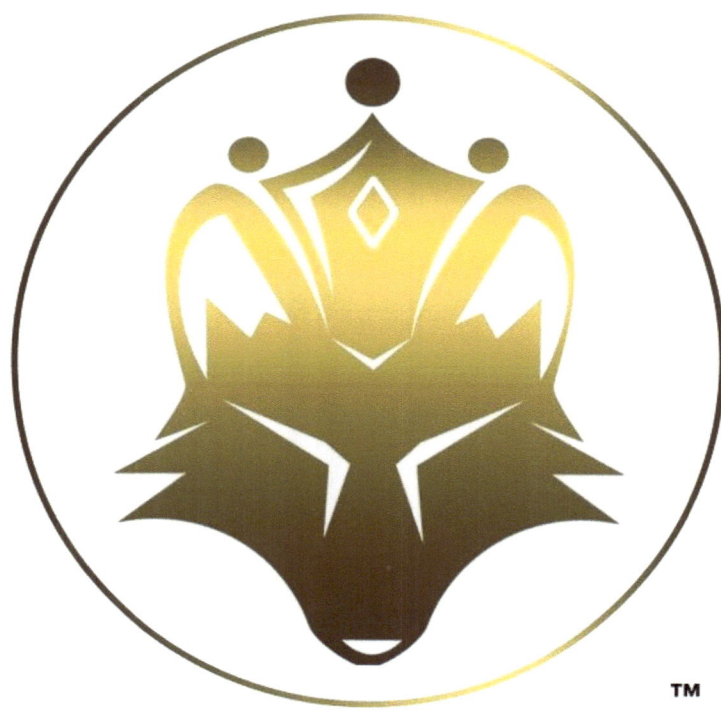

WWW.FOXTAILMAG.COM

FOXTAIL Magazine (ISSN #978-1981-678334), Issue #1 (January 2015), is published bi-monthly by **Foxtail, Inc.**, 945 W. Agatite Ave., Chicago, IL 60640. The subscription rate is $24.95 per year. One-year subscriptions rates: U.S., $24.95; Canada, $54.95; for all other countries, $84.95 in prepaid U.S. funds. Periodicals postage paid at Chicago, IL and additional mailing offices. POSTMASTER: Send address changes to *FOXTAIL Magazine*, 945 W. Agatite Ave., Chicago, IL 60640,. Reproduction or use of any part of Issue #1 (January 2015) of *FOXTAIL Magazine* without the written consent of the publisher is prohibited. Return postage must accompany all manuscripts, drawings or photographs. All manuscripts, drawings or photographs sent to *FOXTAIL Magazine* will be treated as unconditionally assigned for publication and copyright purposes and are subject to the magazine's right to edit and comment editorially. *FOXTAIL Magazine* assumes no responsibility for the advertisements made herein or the quality and availability of the products advertised herein. *FOXTAIL Magazine* assumes no responsibility to determine whether the people whose photographs or statements appear in such advertisements have, in fact, endorsed such products or consented to the use of their names or photographs, or the statements attributed to them. The publisher is exempt from the record-keeping requirements and disclosure statements mandated by 18 U.S. Code, Section 2257 A - C and the pertinent regulations, 28 C.F.R. Ch.1, Part 75, since all of such material falls within the exempted material set forth in Section 75(a) (1-3) of the regulations.

For Advertising Information Contact:
Foxtail Magazine
945 W. Agatite Ave.
Chicago, IL 60640-4044
advertising@foxtailmag.com

FOXTAIL

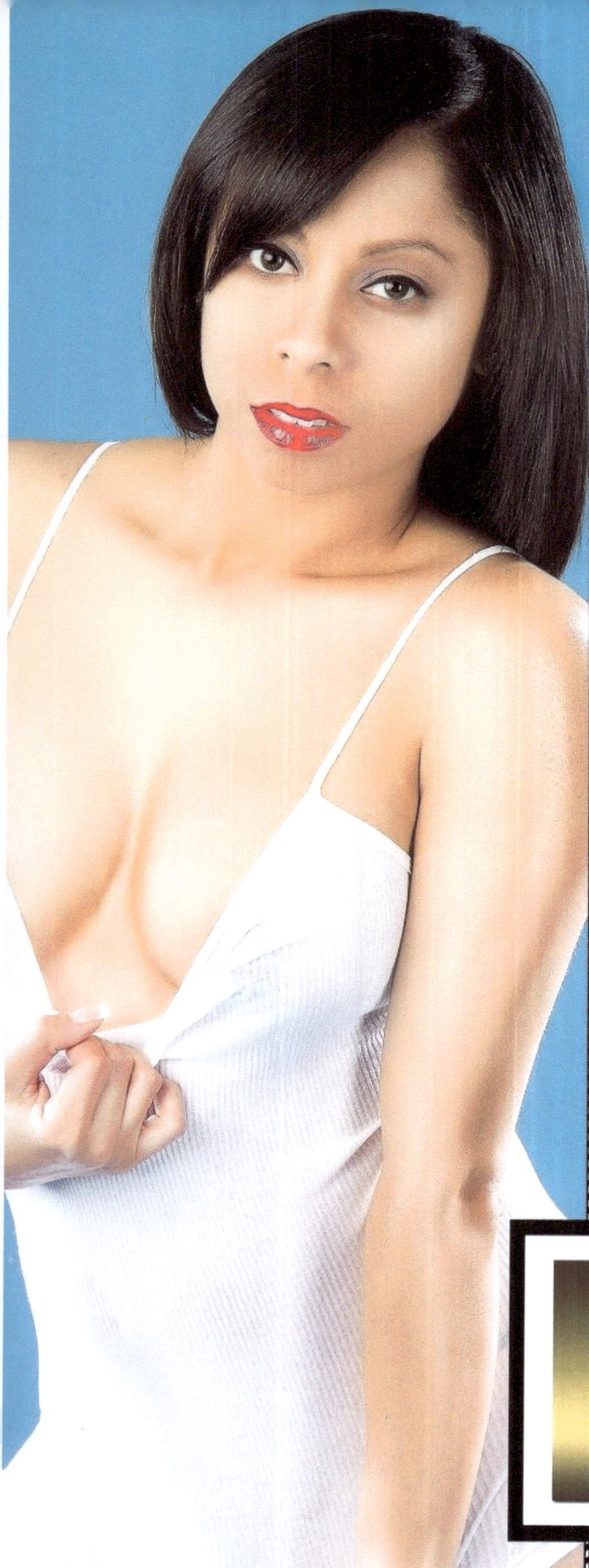

MODEL | TOYA ROCCORD   PG. 24

FOXTAIL MAGAZINE
BEAUTY IS LIFE, AND LIFE IS BEAUTIFUL

EDITOR-IN-CHIEF
Charles C. Rigby II
charles.rigby@foxtailmag.com

ASSISTANT EDITOR
Tony Rudd
tony-rudd@foxtailmag.com

SENIOR PHOTOGRAPHY
Sinovah Kane
sinovakane@gmail.com

GRAPHIC DESIGN/PHOTO EDITING
Sinovah Kane Studios
sinovakane@gmail.com

WRITING STAFF
Erika Jackson
erika-jackson@foxtailmag.com

CONTACT
info@foxtailmag.com
modeling@foxtailmag.com
submissions@foxtailmag.com

FOXTAIL MAGAZINE

WWW.FOXTAILMAG.COM

FOXTAIL MAGAZINE

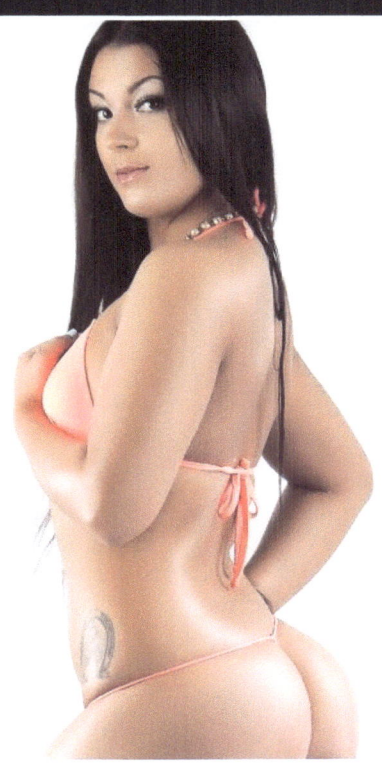

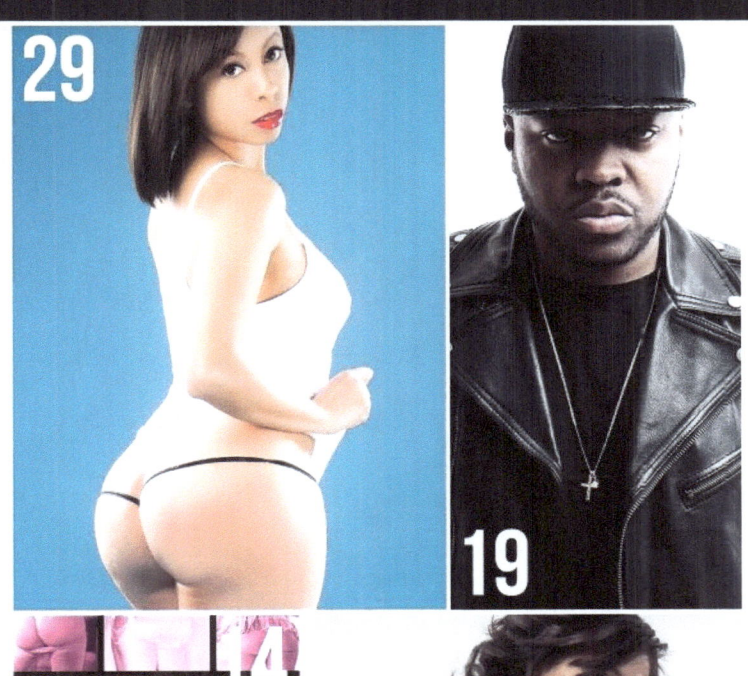

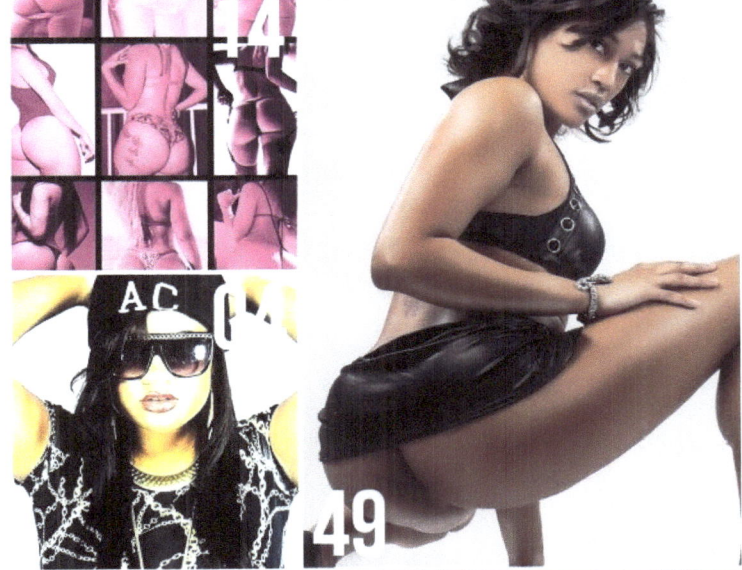

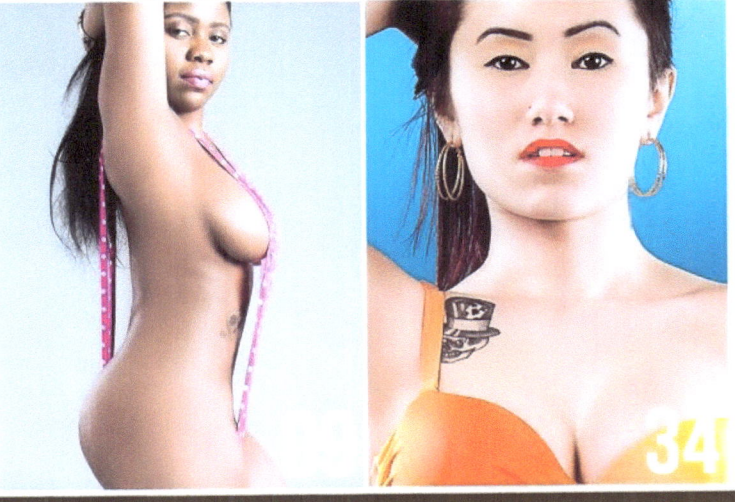

IN THIS ISSUE OF FOXTAIL

DEPARTMENTS
- LOCKER ROOM 04
- LOOK BOOK ..,.. 08
- SHOE PORN 12

FEATURED ARTICLE
- MR. MACNIFICENT: SEAN MAC 16
- THE PHAT ASS PHENOMENON 20
- RIDIN' CHI: AC STYLES 24

FEATURED MODELS
- NU NU 28
- TOYA RECCORD 39
- AYASHE STONE 36
- CASIA JUSTINE
- SHANIQUE HERNANDEZ

THE LOCKER ROOM | *Where All Real Conversations Start*

QUOTABLES

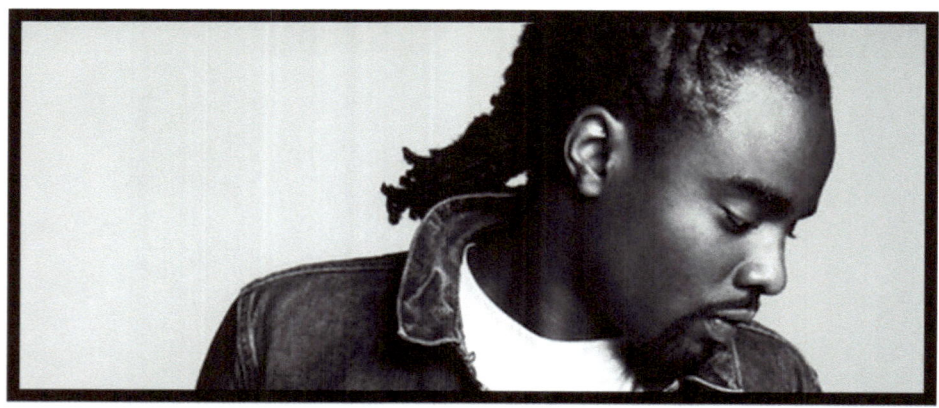

"I carry myself with confidence and humility ., I always try to have a lighter side to MMG.. Cuz I understand I don't "fit the mold" so if I'm tryna spruce an interview up to show that we not tryn be "serious tough guys" on the red carpet Or try to be a bit more engaging to broaden our audience forgive me . I never wanted anybody to think we take ourselves THAT serious. (Were rappers)I don't need to take anybody shine.. Or hate on anybody . I walk in a completely different world .. Where I look for slp jeans and Shanghai dunks online and know what "kayfabe" means. I check nbadraft.net daily . I'm on whatculture allll day I enjoy shyt like that. I play fuckin Zelda and fuck wit bitches who teach yoga and paint... I get it . I'm different . I always embrace that shyt.. I encourage y'all to embrace what y'all like or the person y'all wanna be..."

- WALE *On rap beef between him and labelmate Meek Mills*

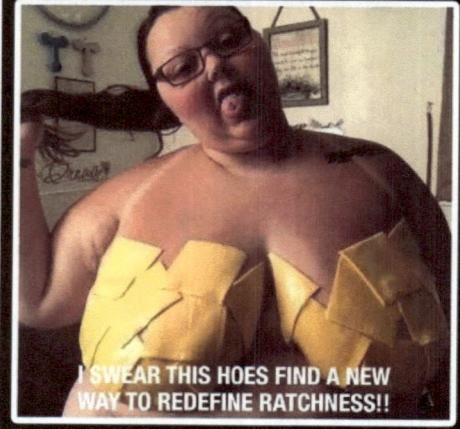
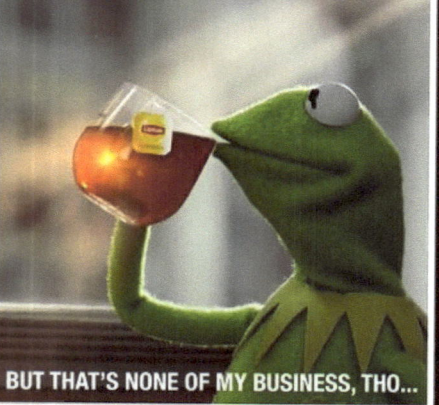

WORD OF THE MONTH

winkler • A non-verbal form of communication used by men and women to initiate a hook-up and/or long-term relationship. The winkler consists of unzipping one's pants and waving one's penis at women until one of the women winks at the man doing the winkler thus confirming the hook-up.

GUESS THE EMOJI

Send your answers to letters@foxtail-mag.com and win a free Fox Candy Girl poster!

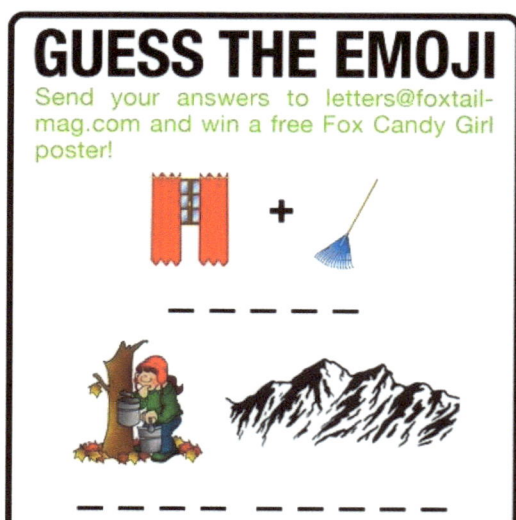

THE PLAYLIST

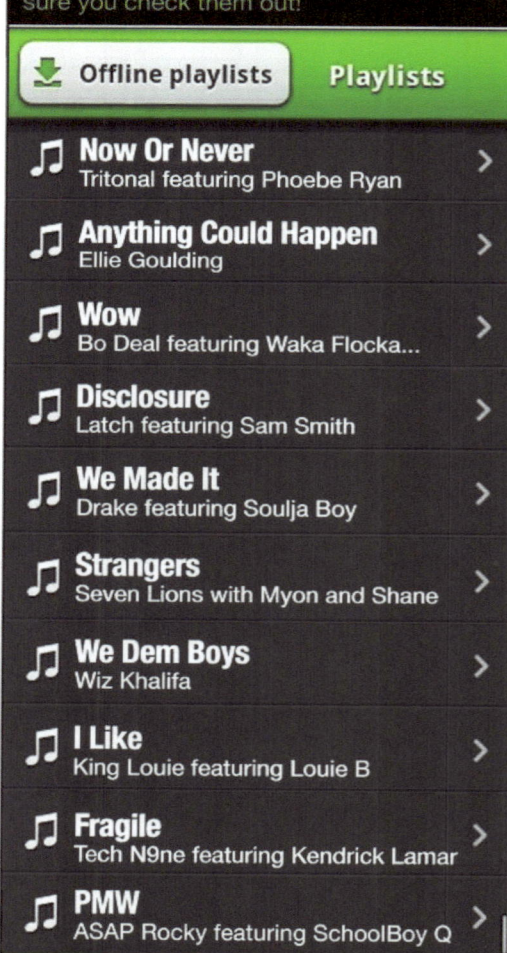

STAY CONNECTED

WITH FOXTAIL MAGAZINE

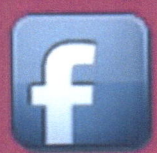 FACEBOOK.COM/FOXTAILMAGAZINE

 INSTAGRAM.COM/FOXTAILMAGAZINE

 VIMEO.COM/FOXTAILMAGAZINE

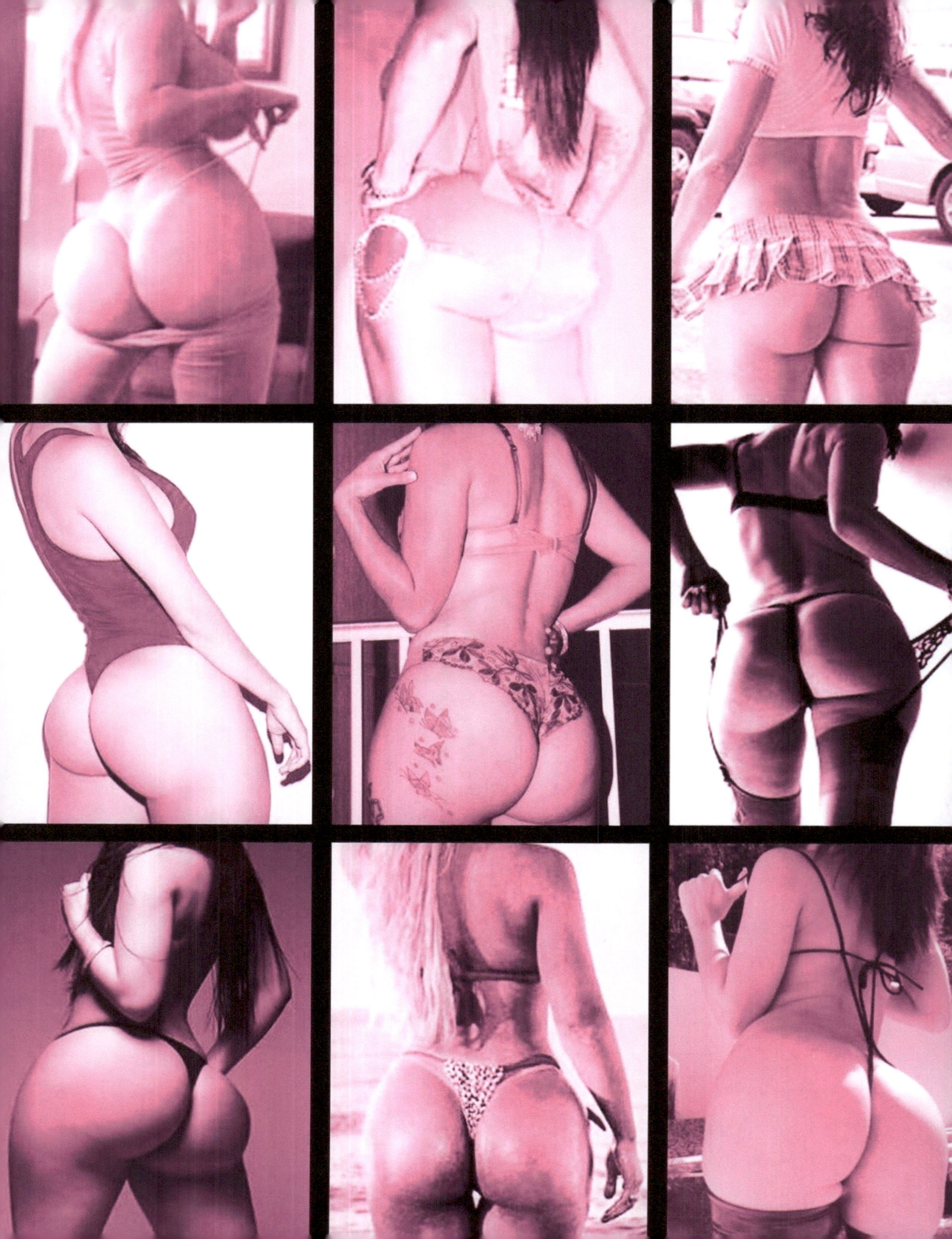

TRUE STORIES

THE PHAT ASS PHENOMENON

by Allura Fox

I was surprised to learn recently that a large number of models want butt implants. I had no idea how important having a big booty had become. And frankly, I'm feeling a little cheated. I feel like I've missed my time to shine. I came to age when the standard of beauty was stick-thin with big boobs. It was a time before Kim Kardashian, when a white girl with a big butt was considered fat, not desirable. It was a time during which my round booty was considered an impediment rather than an asset.

Now, I don't mean to say my ass is huge. An impartial observer, my cab driver the other night, described my ass as juicy rather than big. He said, "I noticed your ass when you got into my cab. It's not like it's real big, but it's juicy as hell. And I'll go ahead and tell you that I'll be watching your ass as you're walking away from my cab too."

But juicy was enough to cause me a lot of suffering in high school. I went to high school when dinosaurs roamed the earth, or the mid-1990s. For my first year and a half of high school, I went to an all white school. I ran track, so my booty was extra round and high. But it was not cherished as it would be today. It was reviled. One boy looked at my butt and said, "That's enough to make my dick shrivel up." As a result, I hated my body. I wanted boy hips, a little booty, essentially no curves anywhere except at my chest. I hid the butt they found so hideous.

My sophomore year I transferred to an "urban" school. My stock soon skyrocketed. I discovered that Sir Mix-A-Lot's "Baby Got Back" was not just a one hit wonder, but an accurate portrayal of black male preferences. I began hiding my booty again, but this time it was because I was embarrassed by the attention.

TRUE STORIES

Despite the accolades from black men, I never appreciated what I had. I wanted to meet the white standard of beauty, so I obsessed about the size of my boobs. White men didn't appreciate a big, round booty until rather recently. Pop culture has exerted its influence over them. And for my white men who have always loved a nice round booty, where were you when I needed you?

So now everyone loves a big butt, but even though current pop culture benefits me, I can't help but think things may be going a little too far. Nicki Minaj has a gargantuan ass and gets a lot of attention for it. There was no one like Nicki Minaj ten years ago. Ten years ago J Lo represented the gold standard, but her butt was big, round, and within the realm of possibility.

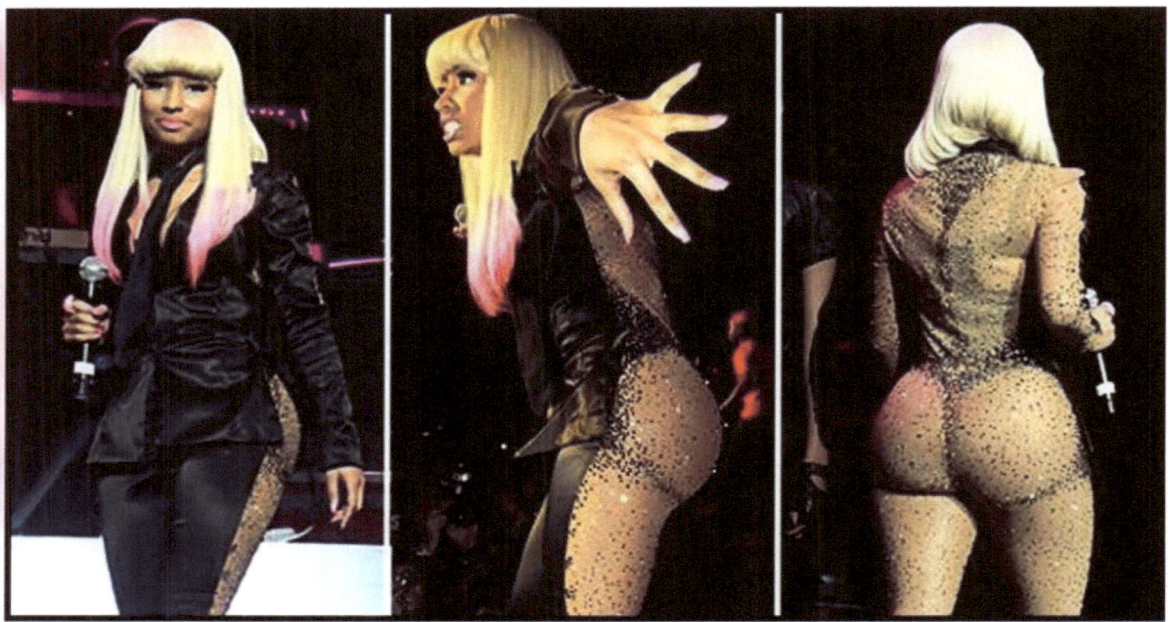

Before writing this, I took a trip down memory lane and watched the "Baby Got Back" video. I noticed that there are only two women in the video who actually had big butts. The others would be considered candidates for butt implants by today's standards.

I'll climb down off my soapbox now and end this column on a positive note. I now embrace my juicy booty. Maybe I can still get in a couple more years of showing it off before I'm officially over the hill. Who knows? With everyone getting butt implants, my butt may be considered small within a few years anyway.

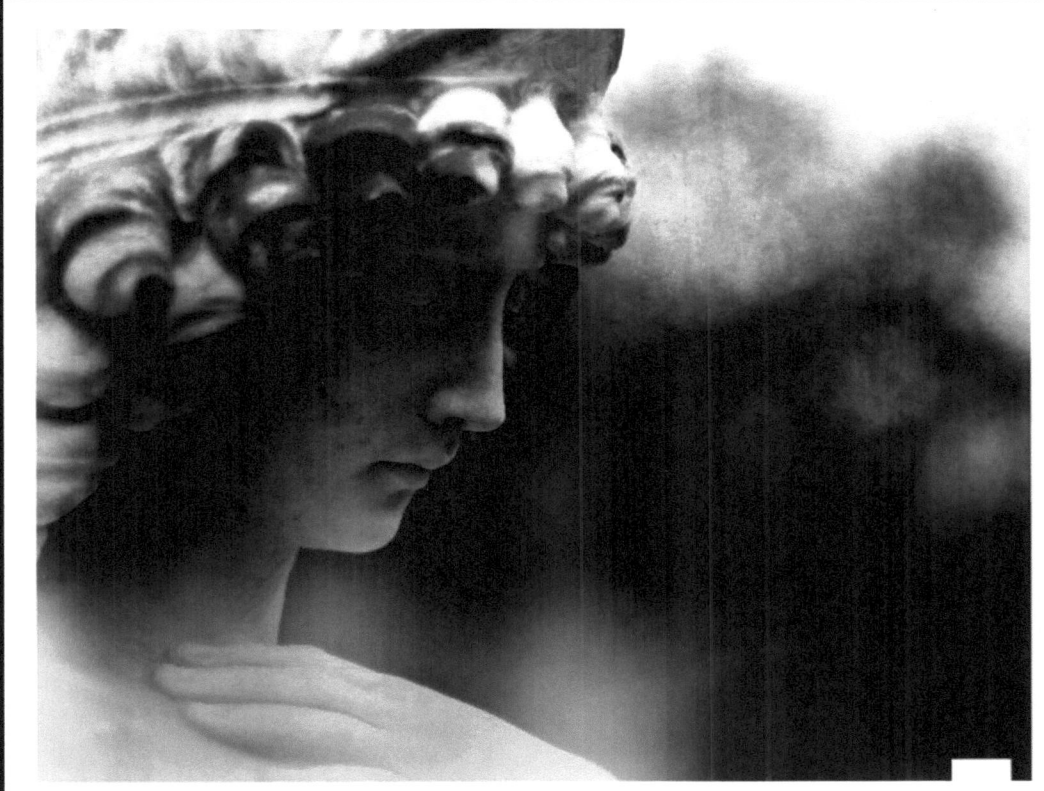

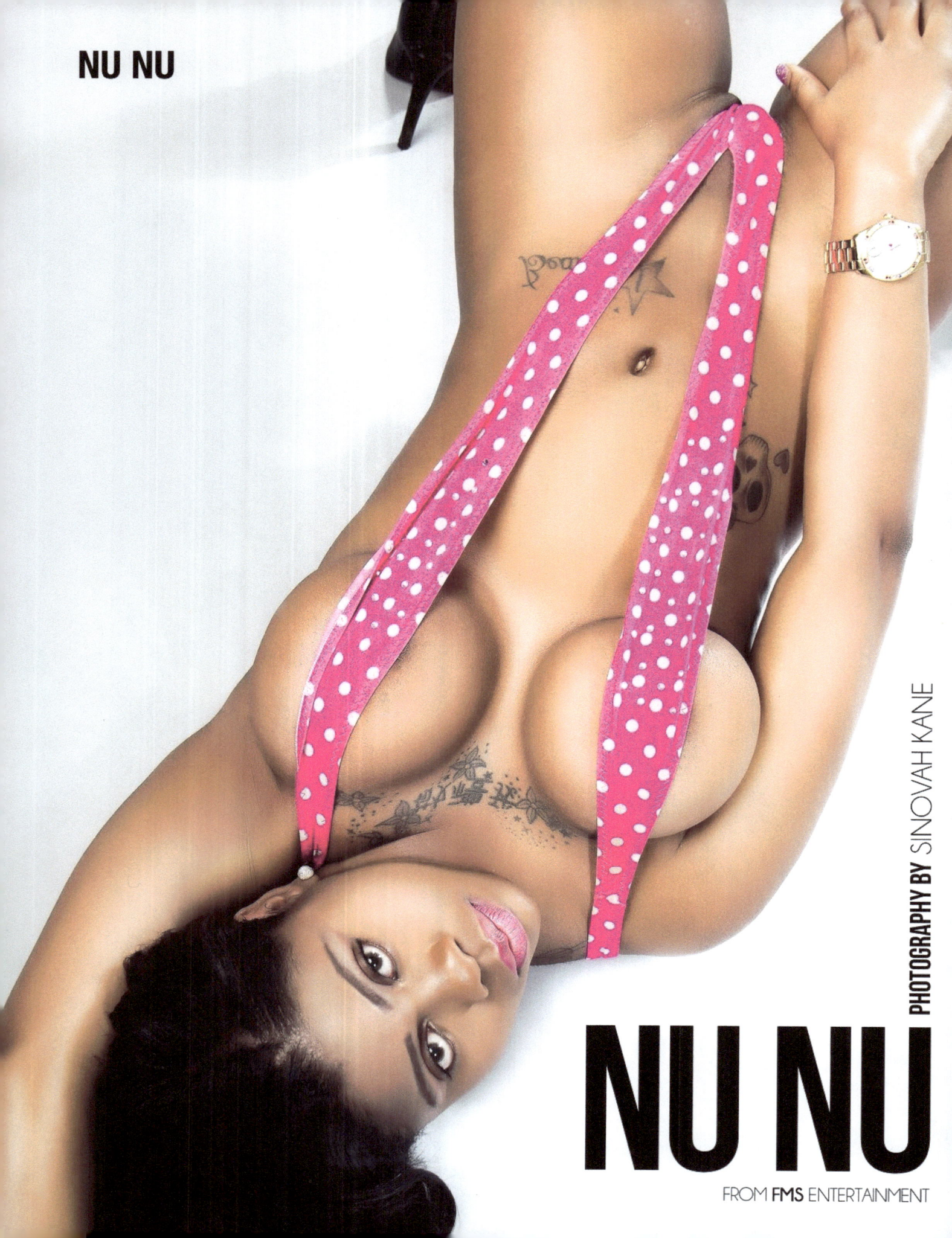

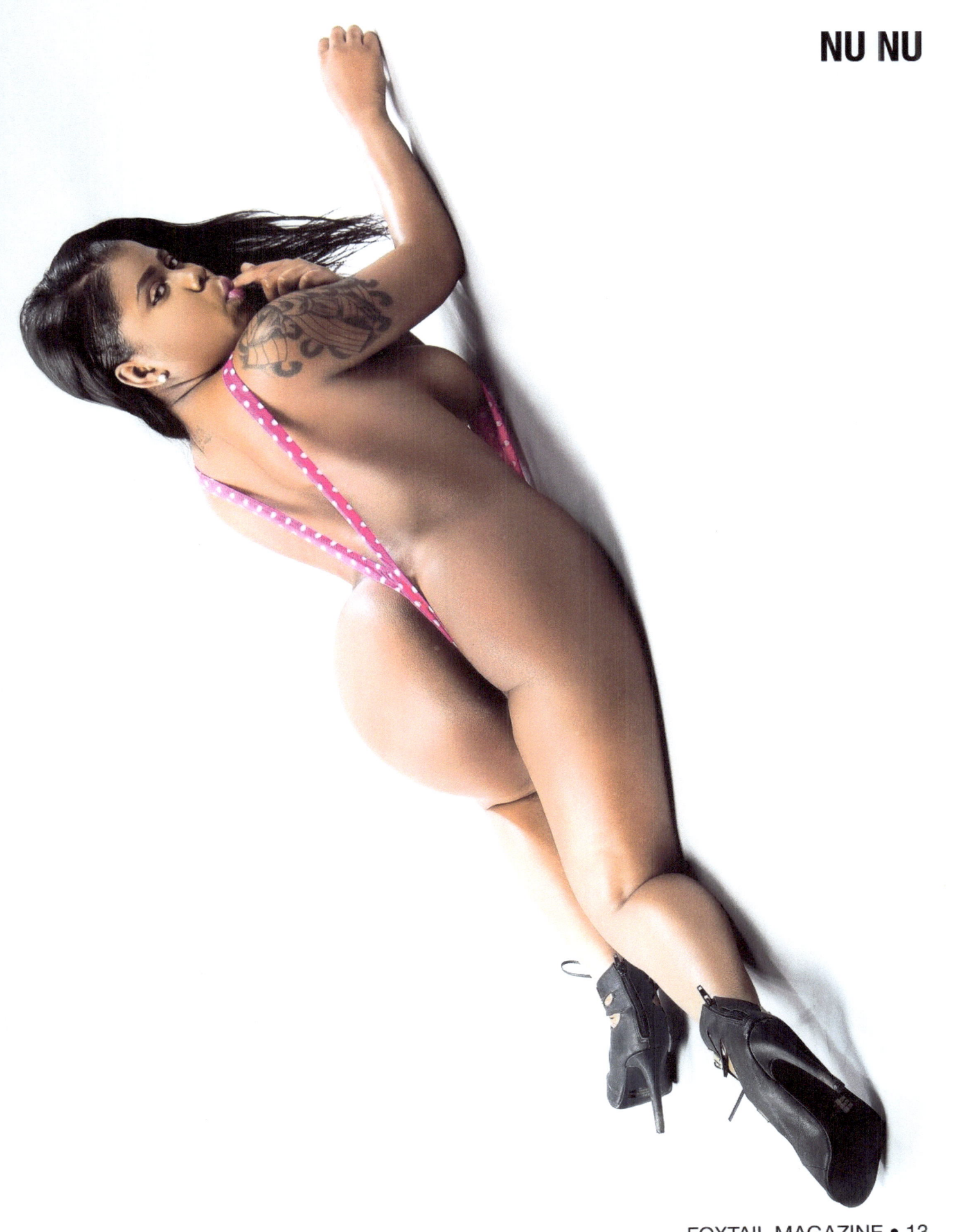

NU NU

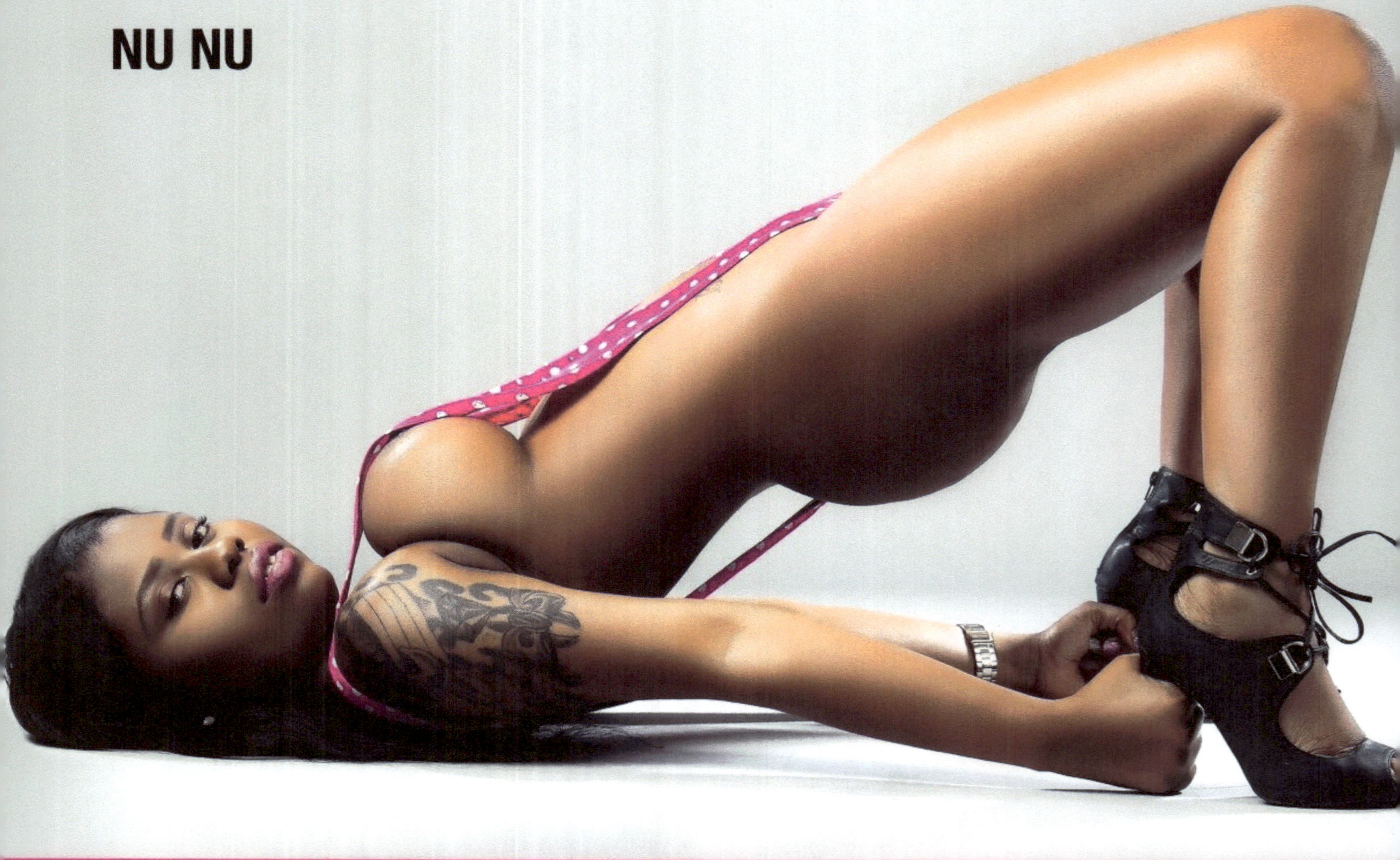

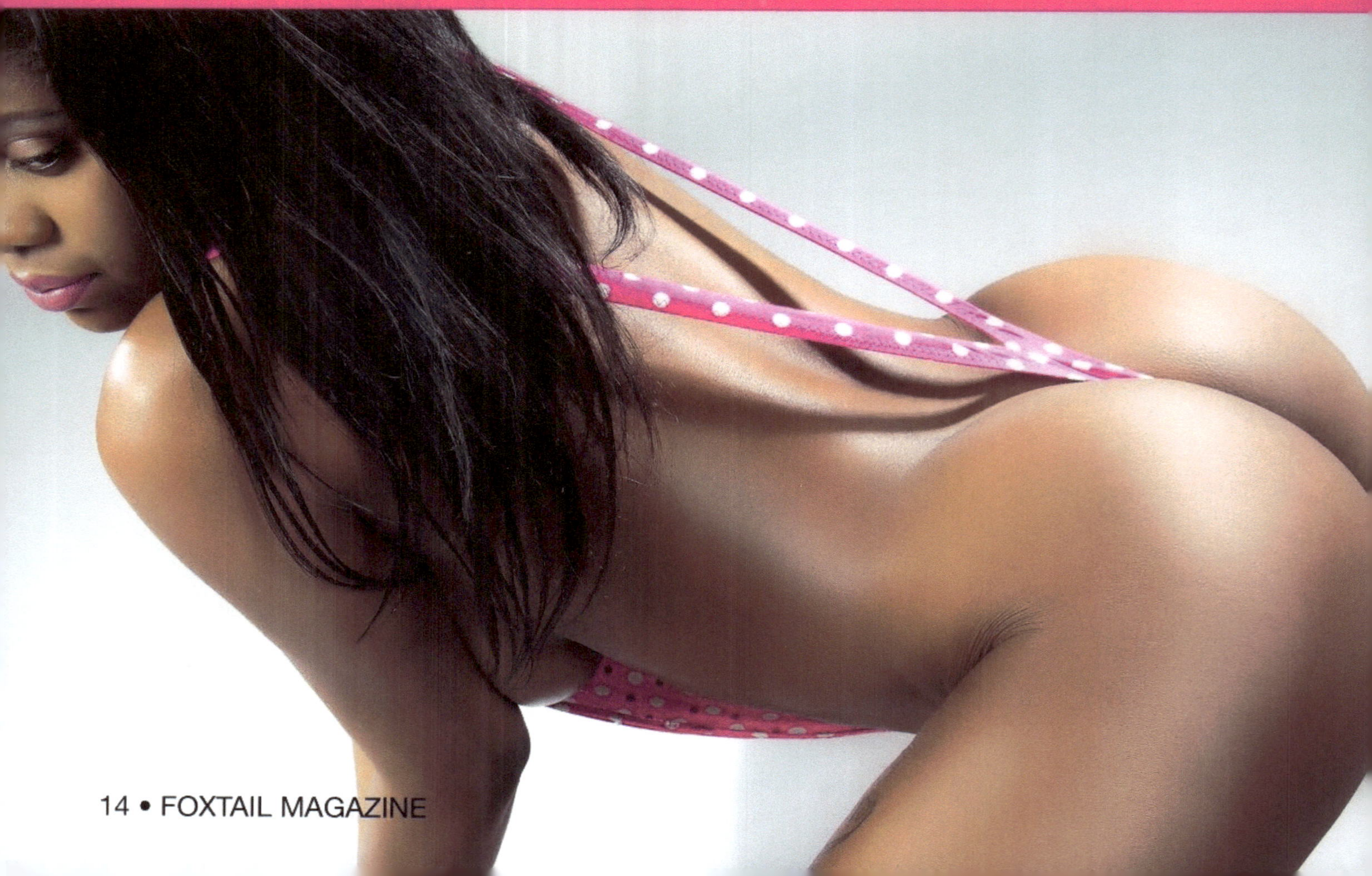

14 • FOXTAIL MAGAZINE

URBAN MARKETING • MUSIC MANAGEMENT • BOOKING AGNECY

I AM 3230

(708) 557-3230 • WWW.IAM3230.COM

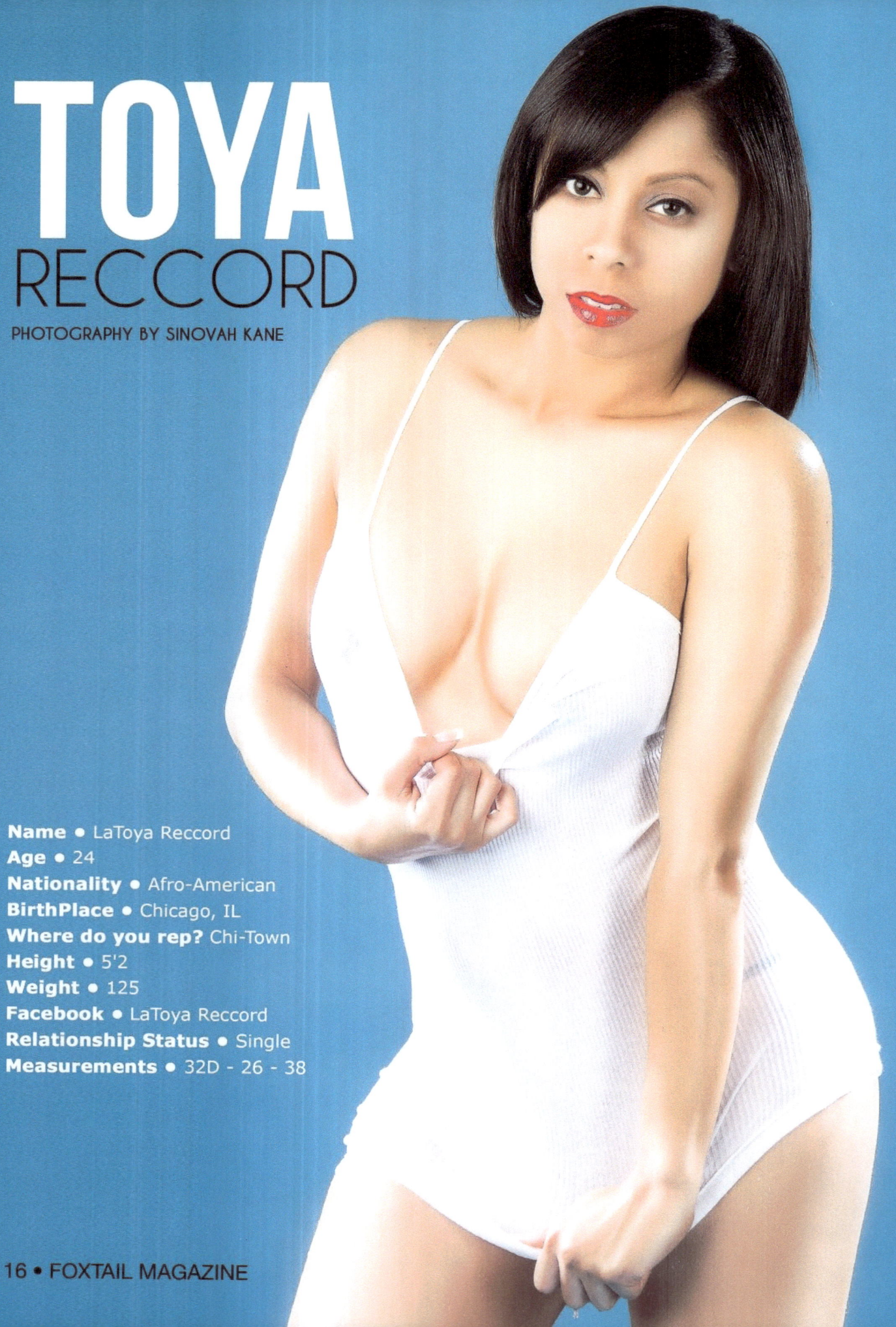

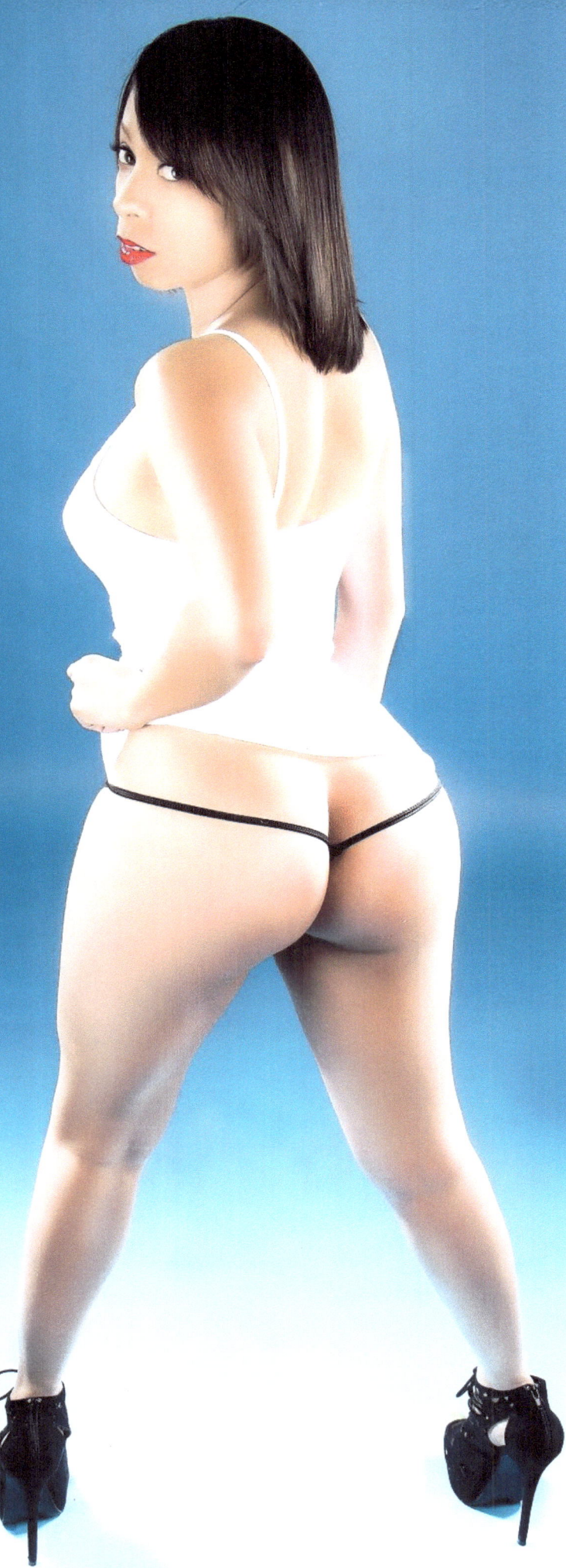

TOYA RECCORD

ALL ABOUT ME!

Would you rather be smart and ugly or dumb and beautiful? Smart and ugly... You can always fix your looks. But, brains are hard to come by, lol!

If you could be invisible, where would you go and what would you do? If I was invisible I will go to the jungle and be one with nature and the animals. I love animals.

Do you consider yourself more of a "giver" or a "taker"? Giver.

What's your biggest turn on? A clean man, meaning good hygiene is a plus!!!

What would the average person say about you? People would say that I'm a true go-getter/hustler, as well as, very nice and passionate about what I do.

What do guys compliment you most on? My smile.

Now, what would you like people to be attracted to? My brains/thoughts.

If a guy doesn't have a lot of money, he'd better have... A brain common sense and a sense of humor!!

What is the sexiest article of clothing you own? Edible panties.

What's your biggest turn on? Broad shoulders, nice teeth lips lol and fresh breath lol.

What do you like best about being a model? The feeling of letting yourself be free physically and mentally.

Do you own any adult videos? No, lol hmmm!

If you were a waiter and a customer was being rude, would you spit in their food? No, but I use to be a waitress, lol. I'd just charge them for every little thing I could, lol. People are so rude.

FOXTAIL MAGAZINE • 17

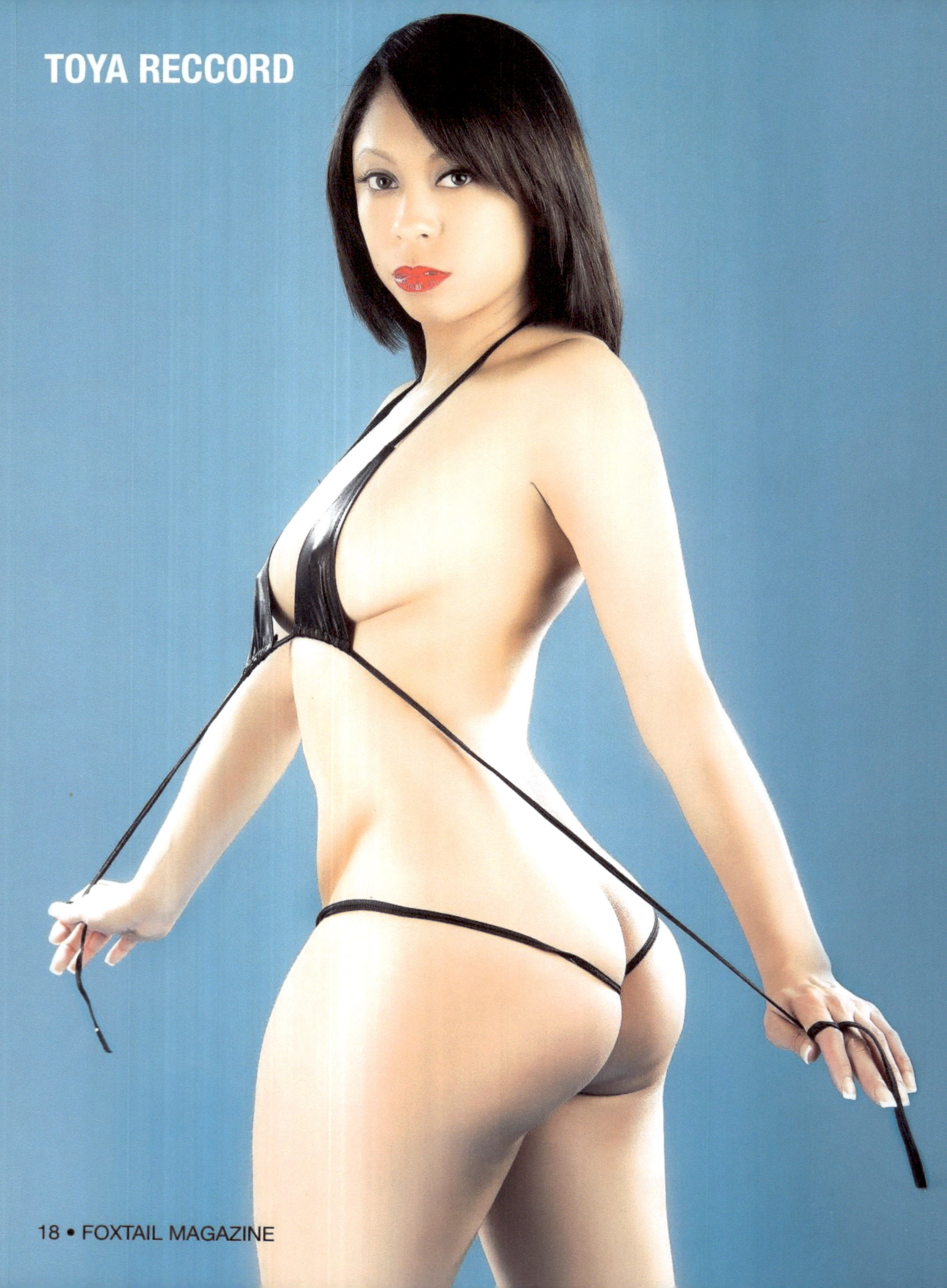

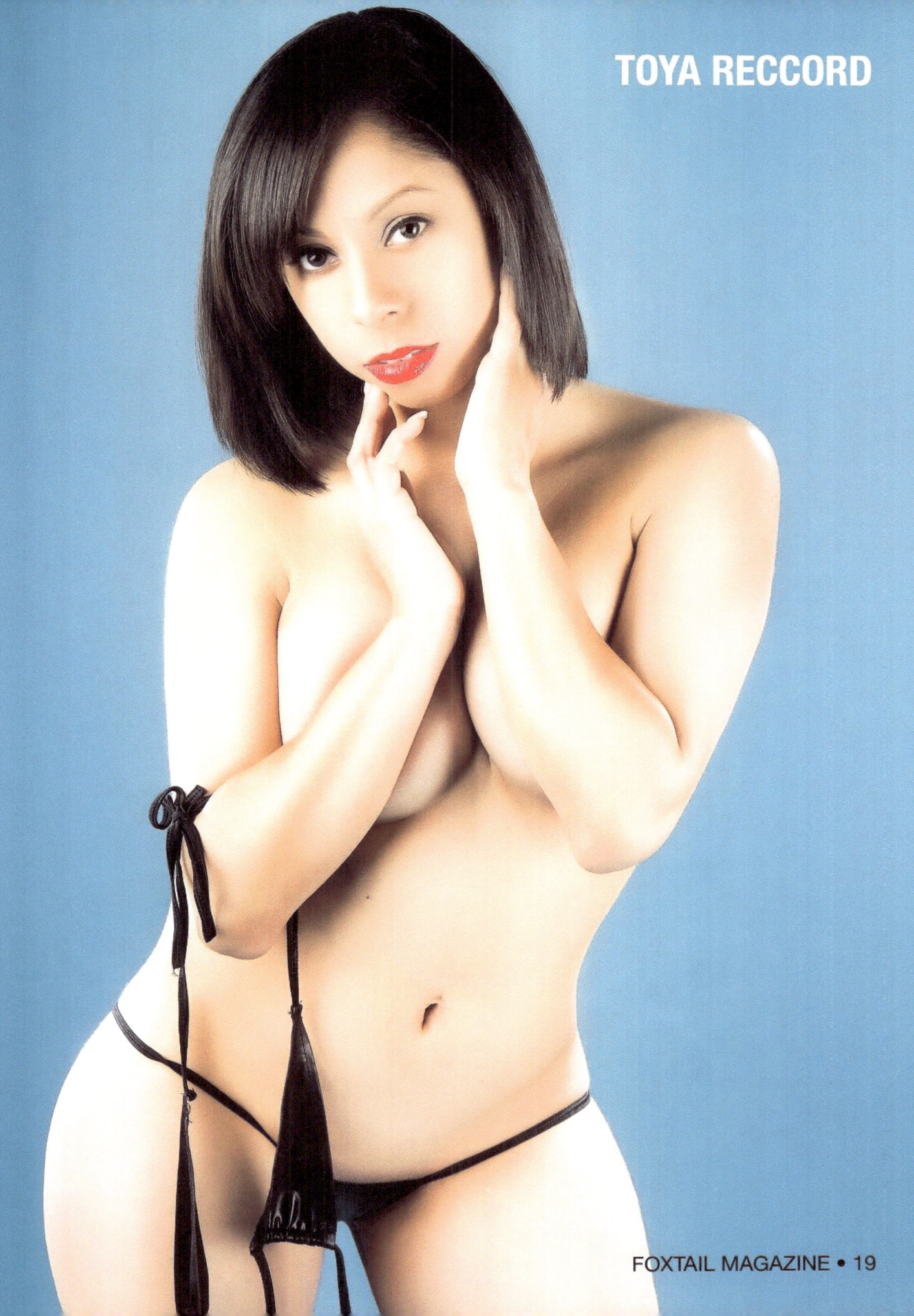

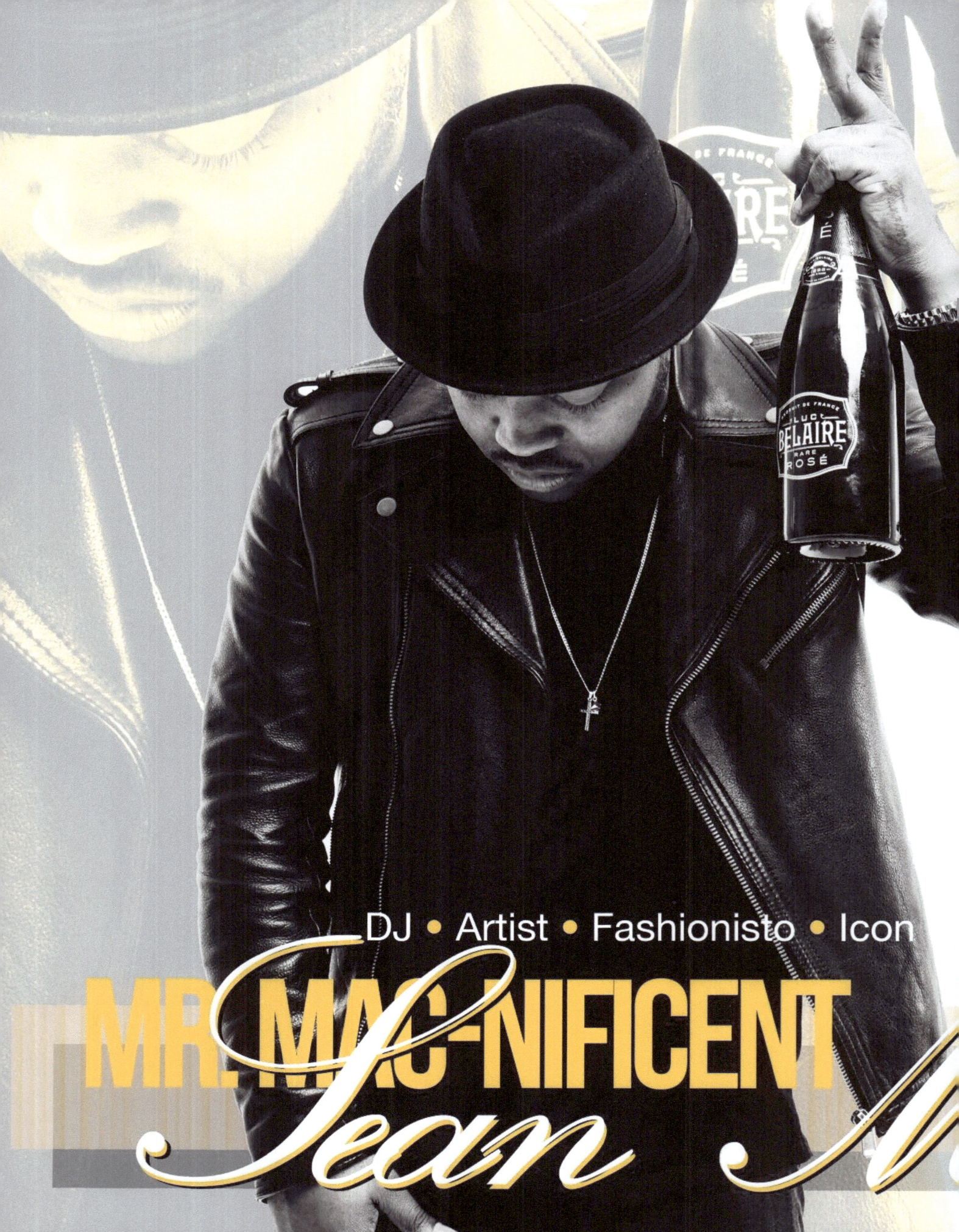

MR. MAC-NIFICENT

BY SINOVAH KANE

FTM: How did Sean Mac get started in the world of DJ'ing.

Sean Mac: I'm 32, so I would say it all started when I was 13. That's when I first fell in love with the art. At 13, I was consumed with everything about New York Hip Hop from sneakers to Gumby haircuts. They worshipped the craft. The rocked show! They brought a pure dope flavor to art of Hip Hop, while at the same time, trying to survive in the streets; and, that's something we can all relate too! I was most inspired by the films like Juice and Style Wars. Juice [The Movie}, though, that was my real inspiration. It wasn't just the movie, I was drawn into the whole culture of DJ'ing. It was Juice [The Movie] that made me really say, "Ya know, that ish looks dope!" It [movie] inspired me to buy some turntables. So, I went out an brought some cheap $20 turntables from the thrift store, that didn't work [laughs]. I got a mixer for my birthday, and I hooked everything up to my grandmother's ol' ass amplifier. Then, I would just be up in my room scratching out a bunch of old James Brown records, you know what I'm saying. That was the whole thing back then.

At 15, I started barbering. Cutting hair kept me busy. Since music wasn't making me money, DJ'ing got the back burner. Around 18, I rolled with DJ Word and DJ Rio, who where really fresh cats. Once again, my friends, fashion, and the culture of Hip Hop inspired me to pick the tables back up. At this time, I didn't want to be something I saw on television. The culture was everything to me. I saturated myself into everything. It was really important to me.. I wanted to be dope, too! That's was it! I started by DJ'ing at 18 and never looked back.

I wanted to come in the game a little different. Every dj has their lane, and I wanted the mixtape and nightclub lane. I started off doing demo for promoters. I found out how was promoting, go home make mixes for them, and come back like… "Yo, I'm dope as hell, check this out! Check this out!" That was back when people were still giving demos to promoters. I was always driven, inspired and creative. It was pretty easy for me to get in the game, you know, because my drive was just second to none. I wanted to be great!

FTM: What do you consider to be the pinnacle moment of your career? What was that one moment that made you feel like, I'm here now?

Sean Mac: Man, I've done B.E.T. eleven times. When I hit that stage for the first time, though! I mean, the flight to New York for Rap City in the Basement, after sending them about 30 press kits, was crazy! I was so anxious to get on that show, especially when Tigger was on there. That was like! When I did that… The phone started ringing off the hook. It was just crazy for me. Next thing you know, I'm playing and dj'ing next to DJ Jazzy Jeff and Kid Capri for the first time, and just absorbing that installation and inspiration was phenomenal. Being on B.E.T., playing next to some of the greatest djs in the world, and being like 21 at the time was all like this is real.

FTM: I've heard something that you like to slam tracks. How would you describe your style?

Sean Mac: Everybody slams tracks. That's the way of the world. Nobody really does their own things, unless like I'm djing Essence Weekend. That's a place where I can be more creatively artistic. Mostly, it just depends on where I'm booked. I'm a Hip Hop DJ, but I play pop, EDM, Ol' School, and house. I love it all! As for cutting records when I cut, sometimes I just slam a record in. Sometimes, I just scratch a record in. Most of the time, I just blend music in. I do a lot of blends when I play House Music, Dance, Pop, or EDM. IT really just all depends.

FTM: That's brings me to another question. What do you think about the whole EDM movement? Are you planning to get into that scene?

Sean Mac: Hell Yeah! [laughs] That's where the game is right now! I have a few friends in it heavy like Flosstradamus. Those are my boys from Chicago. Plus, a lot of cats I look up to and respect in the game are tapping into that market and getting paid. These dudes get like $100,000 a gig, you know what I'm saying! They make like $50,000 for 2 hours. That's real deal! It's a real business. It's a huge market for EDM, right now!

SEAN MAC

FTM: I call it the new 60's, or the modern hippie movement. Peace, Love, and Molly!

Sean Mac: It's a festival type of vibe. The crowd brings out 1000's of people. It's nothing like nightclub parties which is so underneath this. Club parties aren't even on the same level. The money. The business. The energy. It's all a completely different atmosphere. Nothing is the same. Particularly, a lot of EMD DJ's are white. It's just the truth. Most of them are white, and you'll be surprised at the racial barrier that still exists. That burden that some dj's still have to bear. There's just a lot of segregation. Regardless of how well you play pop EDM, mashups, or electro, you're placed in a box when you are black. It is the truth. It has always been the truth. That is going to be the truth forever.

FTM: Well, that certainly won't stop me from getting my EDM on.

Sean Mac: I fucks with EDM. I fucks with it all. I love the energy. I'm an energy DJ. I'm more so like a stadium DJ, as I like to call it. I spin the biggest parties in Chicago. I'm booked for every major weekend from All-star, to the Super Bowl. They call me along side some of the world's most renowned heavy weight DJ's. I'm a representative of that wave in Chicago. But it's not just being that, it's what I'm known for. I'm open to different things. I don't want to cap myself off with just doing one thing. So that's why I do play EDM. I play pop and heavy fist pumping music and get people going crazy. It gets me in a position where people will fuck with me with open arms.

FTM: That's the kind of thinking that opens up a lot of different doors.

Sean Mac: You have to be smart enough to know how to get out of box if you find yourself in a box.

FTM: What do you think are your main challenges as a dj? Do you find anything hard about being a dj?

Sean Mac: I don't know. I have an all around balance. I'm a master mind with the mcing. I'm sick with the blends. I feel cool. I'm in a good place with a good balance.

FTM: Have you ever considered going into production, or have you produced?

Sean Mac: Funny thing is, I've laid hooks for people. I've executive produced records. I have a master ear for hearing the next major hit. That's why most artists work with me. I never went into production because my plate was so full with things I've been accomplishing. So, I just never really got into it. It's another lane. Most DJs become producers. When they do, they lean more toward production than anything. Which to me, is like learning how to do something all over again. Having an ear for something is one thing, but taking yourself back to mental school for something new is just another level.

FTM: What do you usually start with when you're preparing for a set?

Sean Mac: I start by reading the crowd and focusing on where I'm at, and get a feel for what's going on. If the DJ, prior to me, is doing his/her job correctly, I'll know this is what it is, what kind of crowd I'm playing to. Then, I just open my computer up, and I kind of just go in. I have props that I play. I got tags and drops like from Rick Ross and other celebrities, for example. When I come in the building, people know it! Like ayo...

FTM: It's bout to go down!

Sean Mac: It's showtime! I got this dope ass drop from the boxing announcer, Michael Buffer. "Let's Get Ready to Rumble". I go and make a straight move. It's like parties are changed after I like touch those turntables.

FTM: Do you have groupies?

Sean Mac: [laugh] Yeah! [laugh] Yeah, I guess. I'm not too fascinated with groupies. I'm more concerned with entertaining them. I love the fact they follow me and rock me, but that's as far as it goes. Groupies will fuck your shit up, yo! You got to be careful.

What is the future for the Sean Mac brand?

Well, right now, we're talking about radio. Plus, I create fashion. You probably don't know that.

You mean you design clothing or something?

Sean Mac: Well, yeah. I have a clothing collection. I'm a fashion aficionado. It's called Casket Collection. Casket 33 A.D. It is a street wear brand. I design collections once a month. The web store opens up when I drop new collections, for a limited time. Then we close the store. You can go online at casketcollection.com. You can also find us on instagram and twitter. Also, by next year, I will be working on my first single. This will be me working on my artist.

FTM: You mean as an emcee?

Sean Mac: Nah, nah. I'm putting huge records together like DJ Khaled. I'm bout to work on my single, the Sean Mac single. It will have somebody like Young Thug and King Louie, or something.

FTM: That would be hot, I would love to see it. Do you have any other up coming or current projects?

Sean Mac: Check out my SoundCloud at DJ Sean Mac. I have two projects that I do, which drop every couple of months. One is a mix series called "Trap Vs. Drill". Which has done really well. And, I have a new series, it's going to be called, "Just Make the Girls Dance". This whole different entity of work. This is going to be more so catered to women.

s always
n, inspired
ative. It was
easy for me
n the game,
ow, because
ve was just
d to none."

- an Mac -

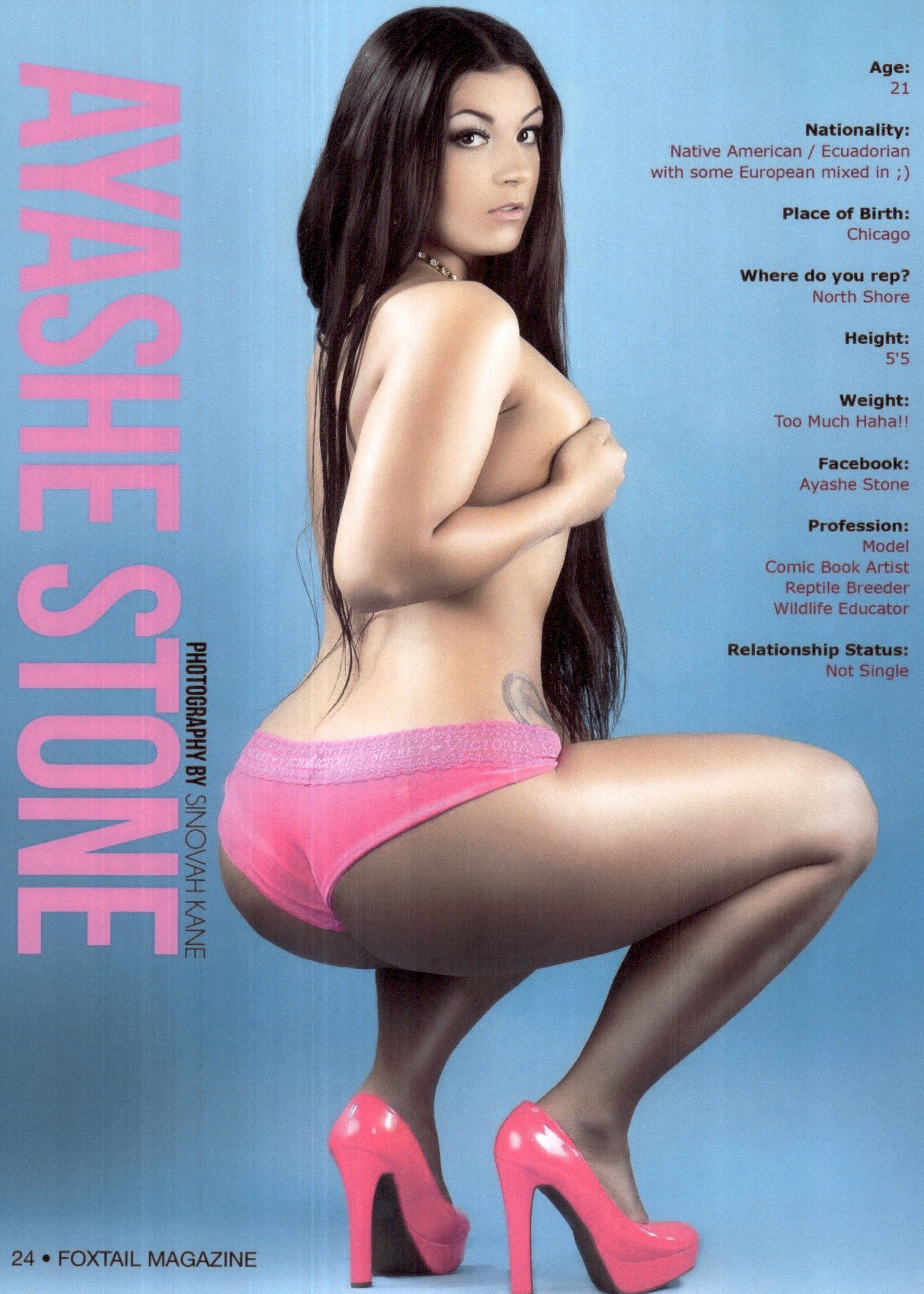

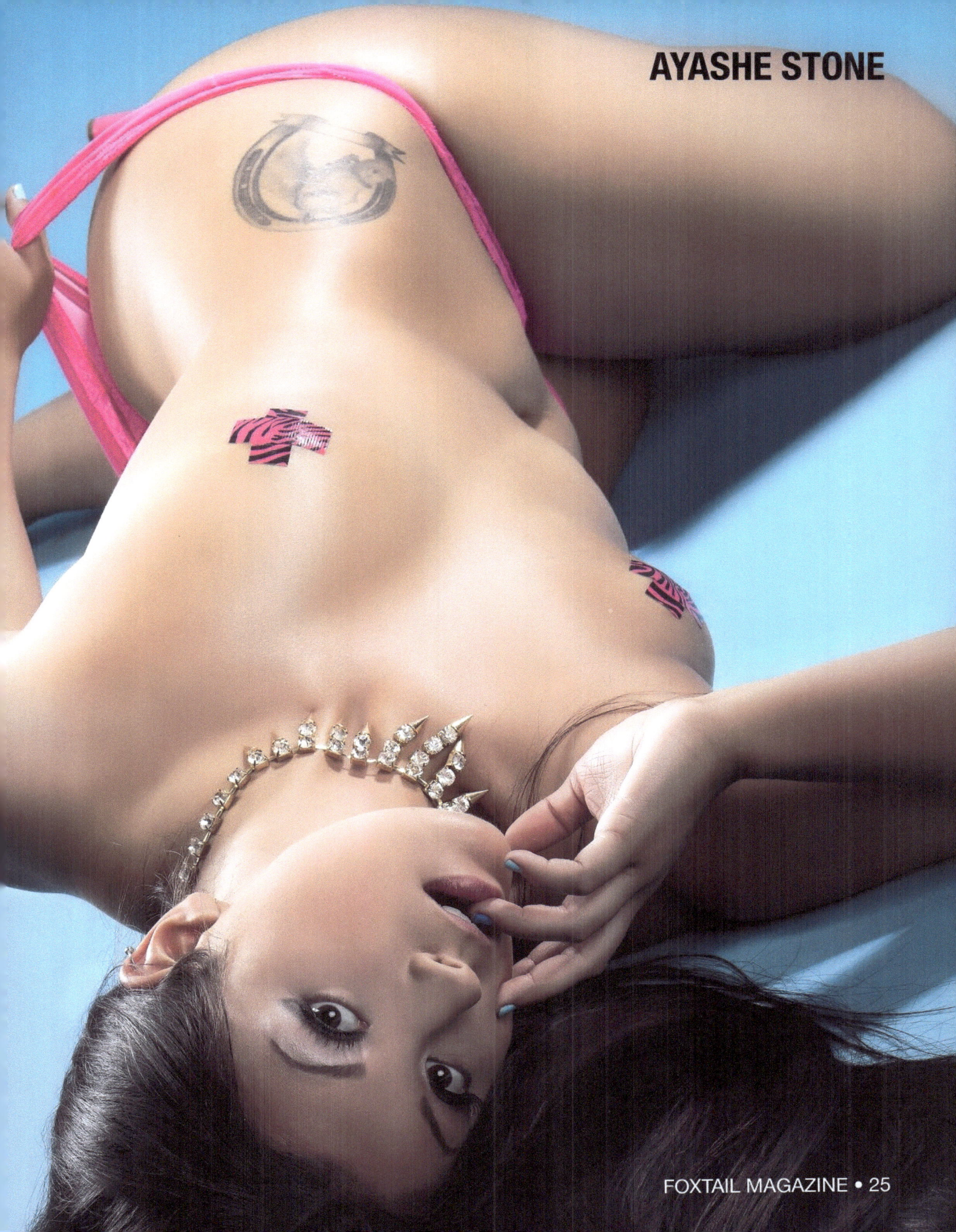

AYASHE STONE
ALL ABOUT ME!

What's the worst lie you ever told? Did you get caught? *Hmm... Not sure if I should go there!*

Would you rather be smart and ugly or dumb and beautiful? *The first one absolutely! Brains > Beauty.*

If you could be invisible, where would you go and what would you do? *I would rescue animals from people who shouldn't be keeping them. I'd probably give em' a good kick in the butt while I was at it. Also - free movies at the theater!*

Do you consider yourself more of a "giver" or a "taker"? *A taker, haha, I take in all kinds of stray, sick, and hurt critters.*

What's your biggest turn on? *173rd AIRBORNE & Roughness!*

What would the average person say about you? *They woud say I have a lot of interesting hobbies, and that I'm crazy for working with venomous snakes and all kinds of wild animals.*

What do guys compliment you most on? *Dat ass, of course!*

Now, what would you like people to be attracted to? *I'd like people to be attracted to each other the way they look normally. Not everyone looks like a porn star.*

What is your Fetish? *Hypnosis.*

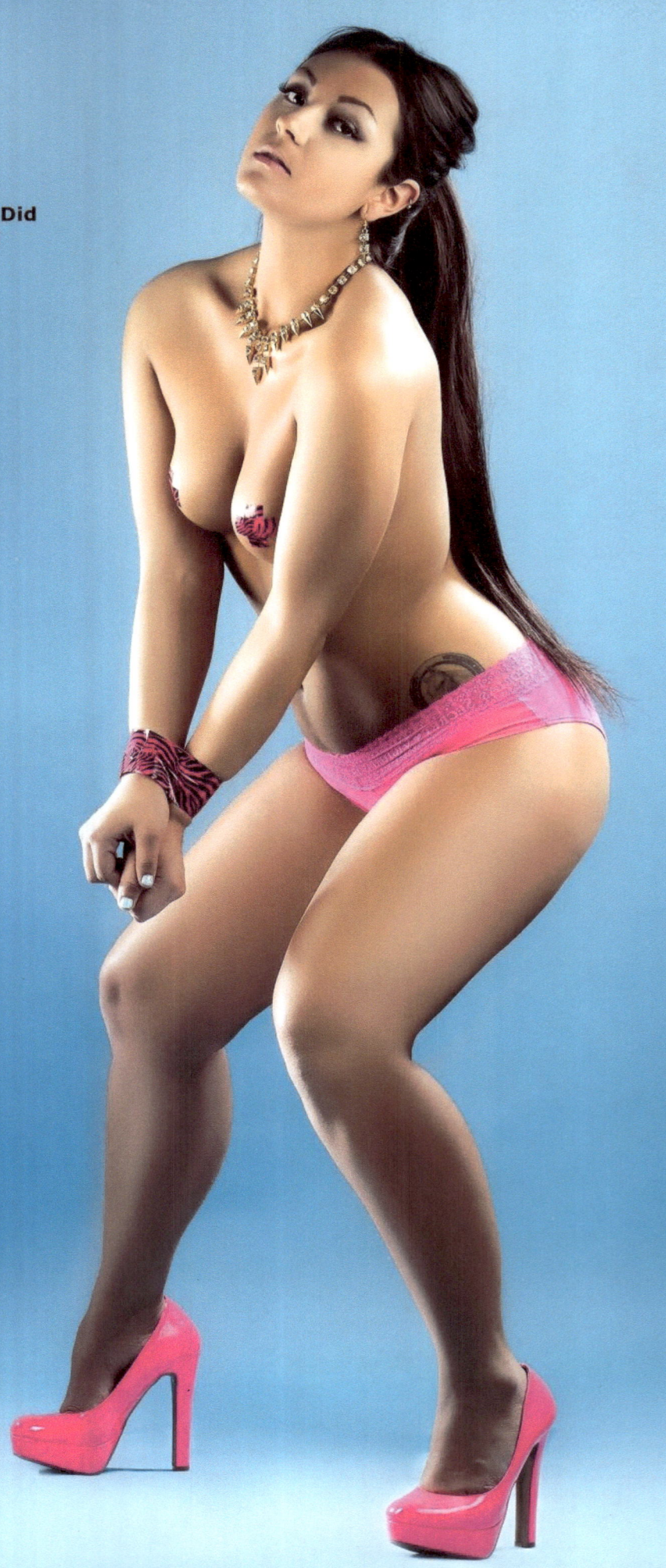

AYASHE STONE

If a guy doesn't have a lot of money, he'd better have... *smarts and wit!*

Have you ever had a one night stand? Details? *No, no, no! I'm not that kind of girl!*

What is the sexiest article of clothing you own? *Pasties ;)*

If you had to sleep with a woman, who would be and how would you get her in bed? *Oh Dear Lord, there's too many for me to choose one. I'd say Selma Hayek and I'd bring her a Burmese snake and ask her to dance with it! :D*

What do you normally sleep in? *Blankets.*

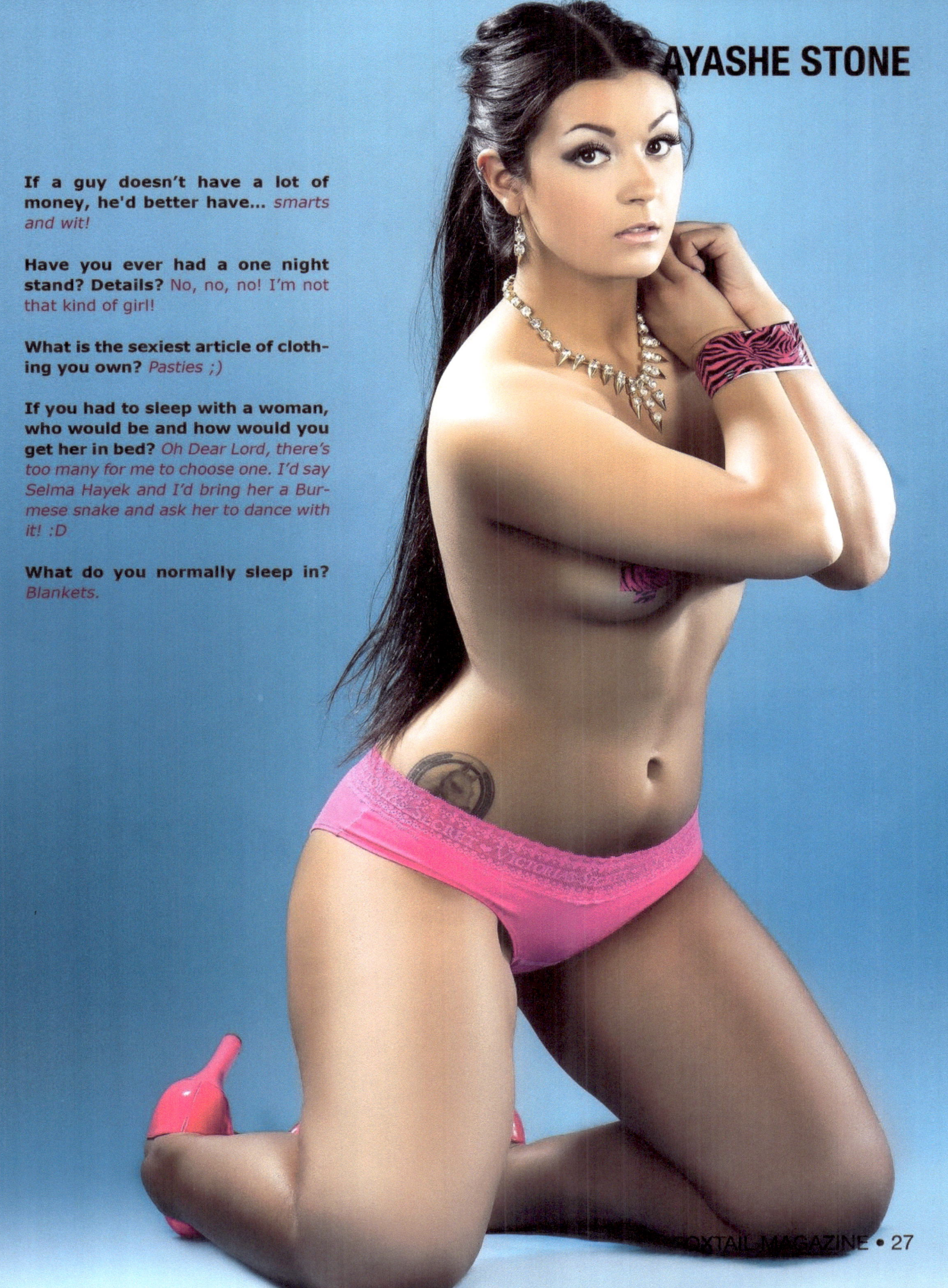

AYASHE STONE

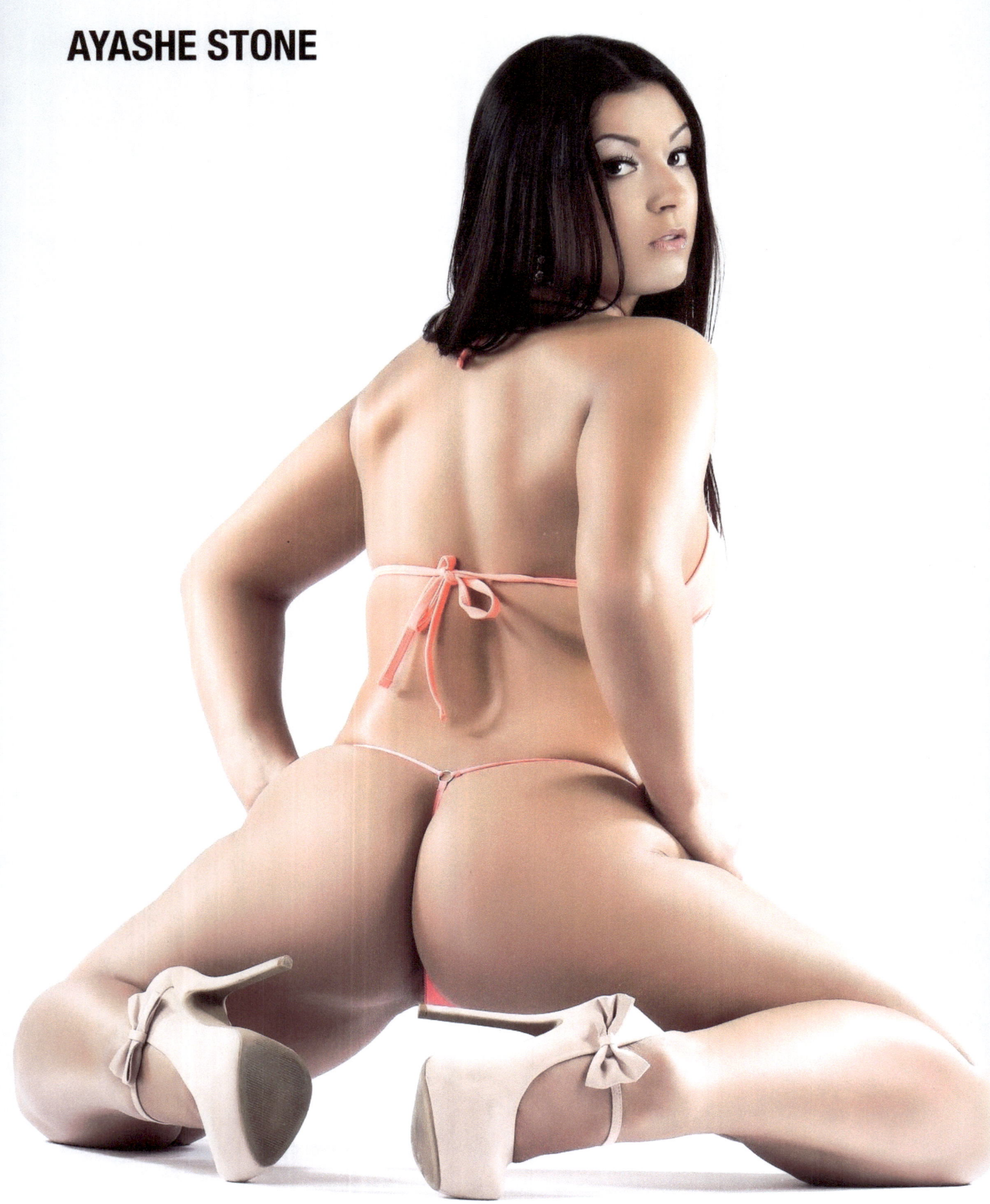

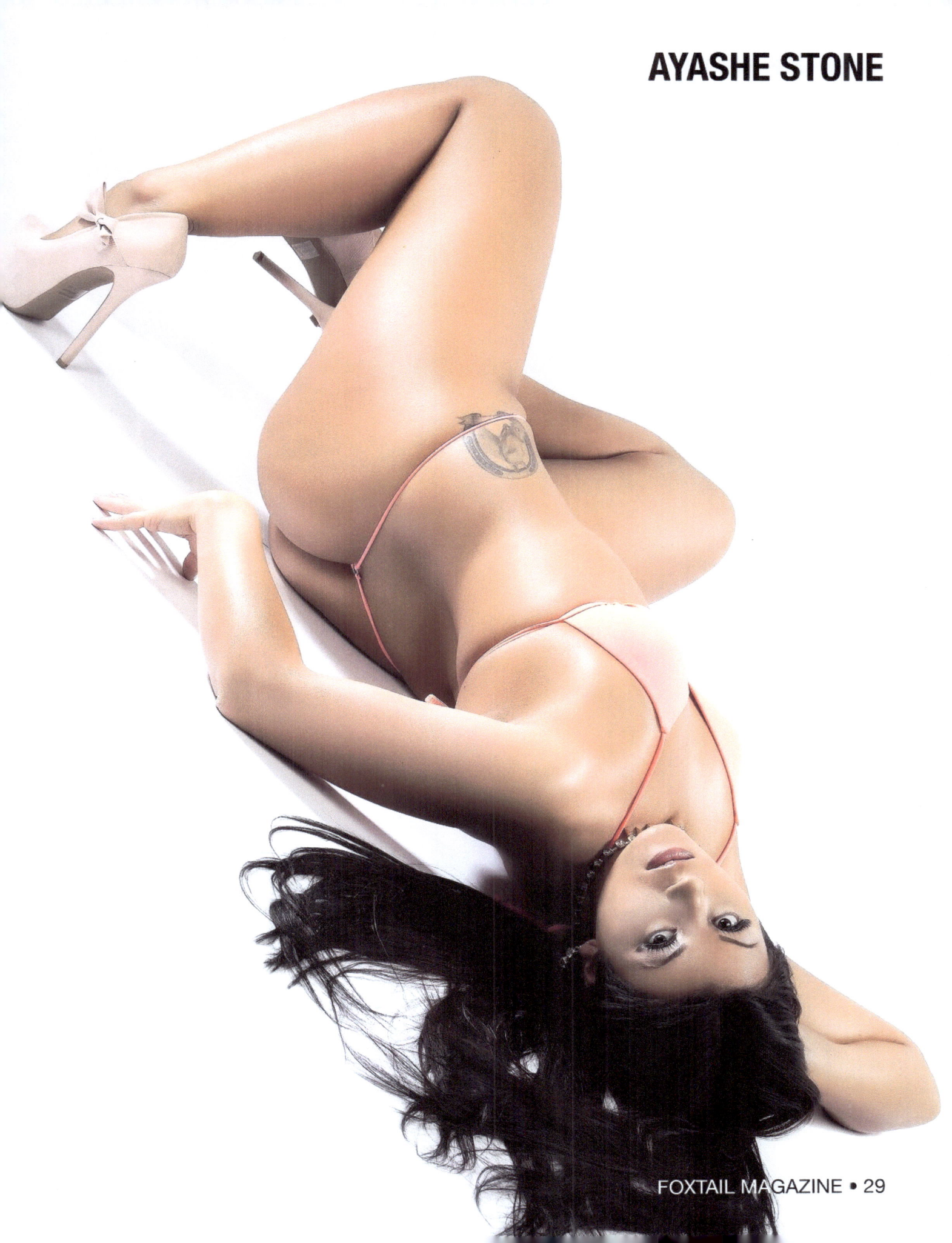

AYASHE STONE

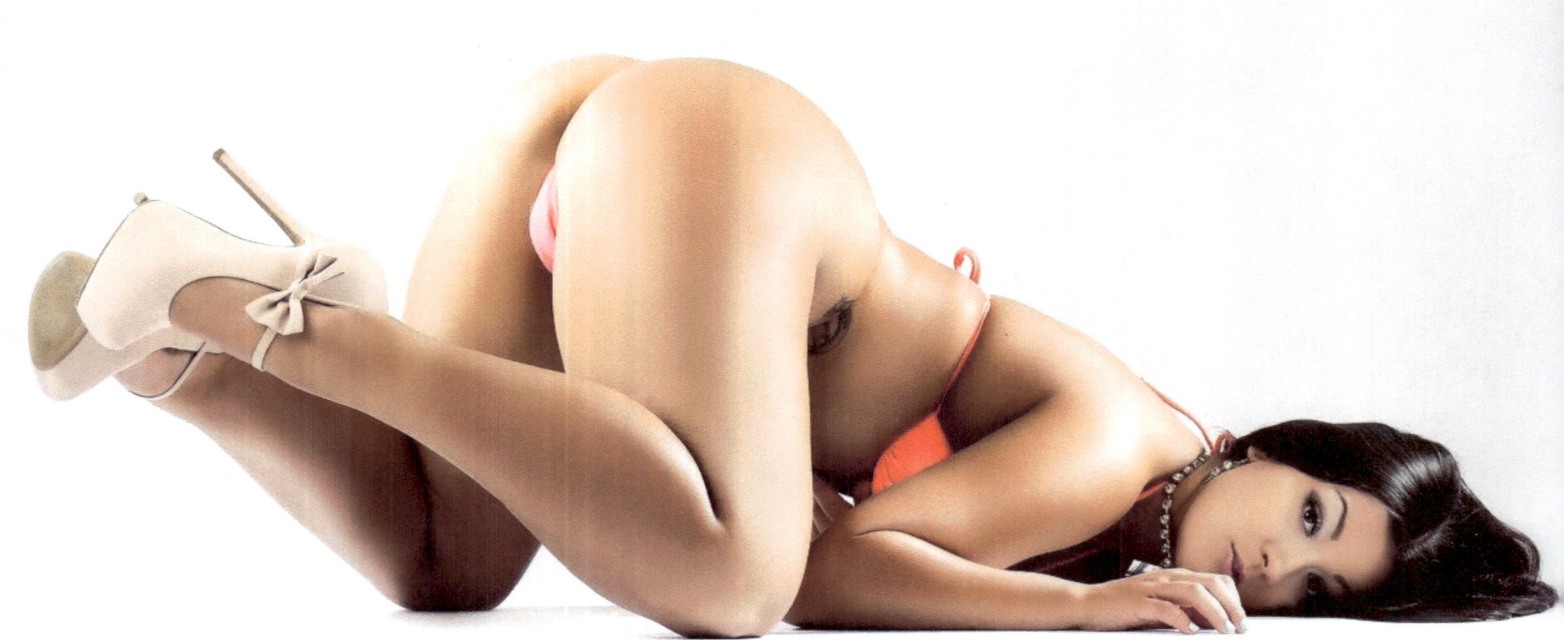

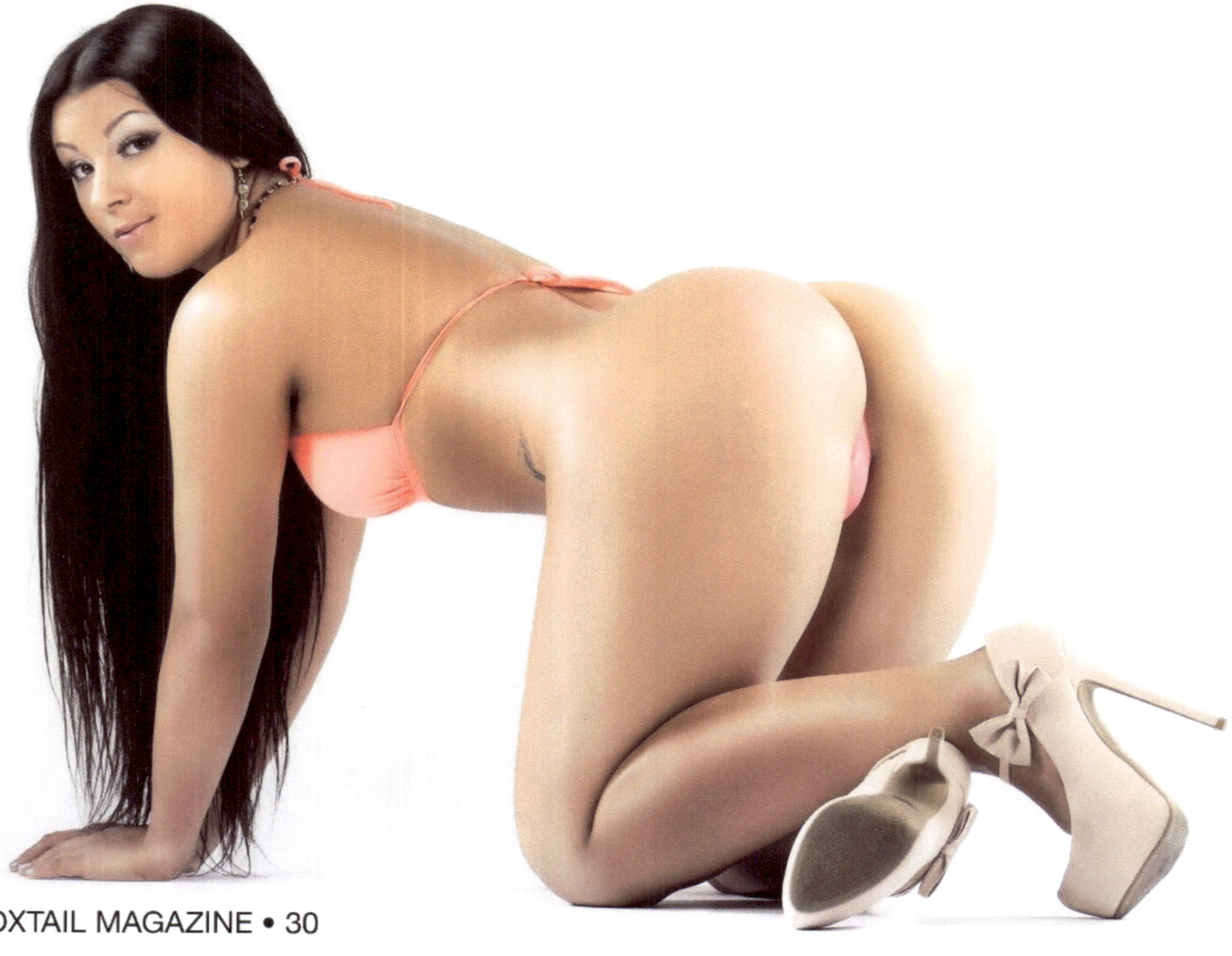

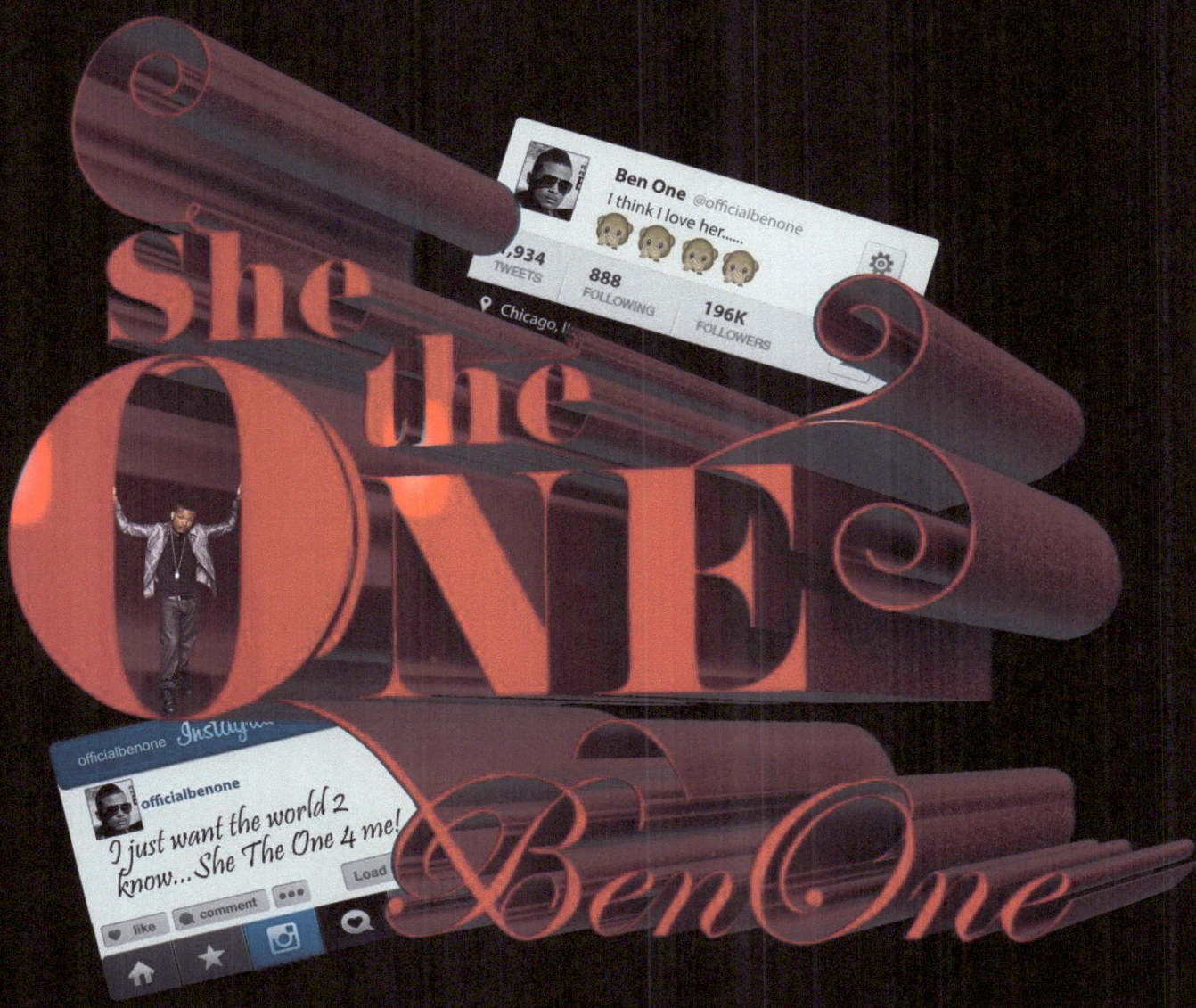

TOP 10 BEST WORLDSTAR HIP HOP HONEY VIDEOS

Let's face it, WorldStarHipHop is killing the game for eye candy videos right now! I mean seriously, many of these videos are directed by some of Hip Hop's elite video directors, and they are giving these beautiful ladies the full-service treatment. To keep it real, WorldStar had very humble begins. They pretty much started WSHH Honeys with low-rent strippers and camera phone videos.

Trust me, they have come a long way. With the success of their site as a whole, the level of girlie videos have accelerated by leaps and bounds. Videos that were once shot in apartment bedrooms and bathrooms, are now being filmed on location at some of the world's most exotic destinations.

I don't really remember the first video I ever saw. I do know that some of these video have been absolute hits while other have been definite misses. Either way, WSHH Honey videos have inspire me to jump in the director's chair and become a WorldStar, myself! I just hope when I finally take the reigns, I can be as half as good as my predecessors. Therefore, as a way to pay homage to WSHH Honey videos, I have compiled a list of what believe are The 20 Best WorldStarHipHop Honey Videos to every bless the Internet.

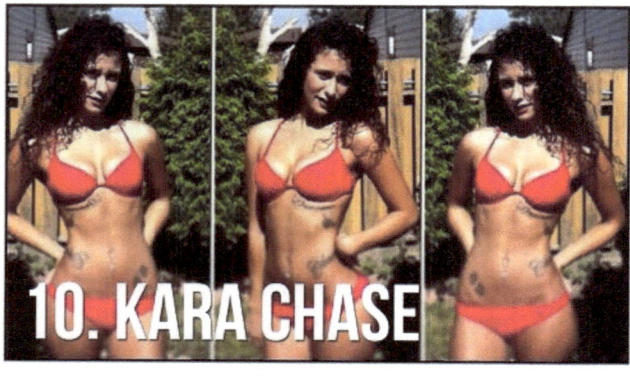

Instagram: prepcesss | Vine: Kara Chase – Prepcess | Music By: Just Blaze x Baauer – Higher (ft. JAY Z) | Directed By: SlaveLaBour | Best Thing About Video: I would chase that ass anywhere!

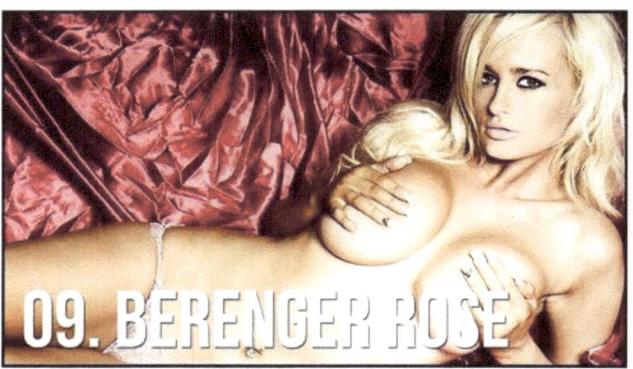

Instagram: Berengerofficial | Music: Hippy – Sabotage | Directed By: Chris Jonez | Best Thing About Video: Those E-Cup are nothing to play with… What am I saying, we would love to play with those E-Cups!

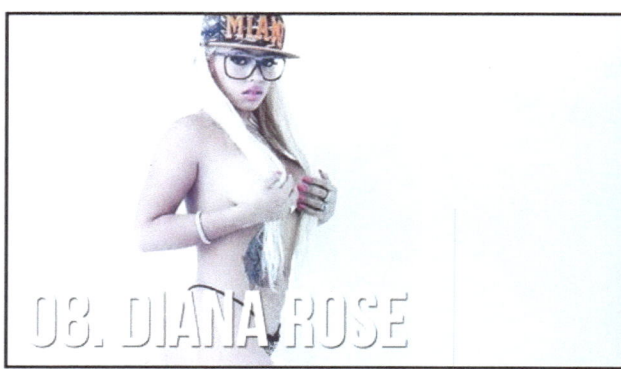

Instagram: BarbieDiabla | Twitter: @BarbieDianeRose | Music By: Jeremih – Ex To See Directed By: @JadaStackkz | IG: JadaStackkz | Best Thing About Video: This yellow model chick got ass and tits that won't quit!

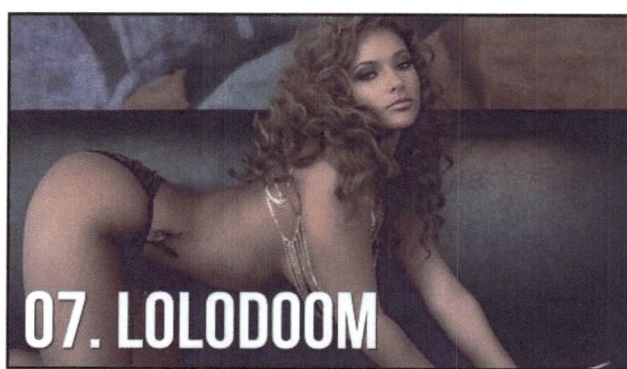

Instagram: Lolodoom | Music: Drake – Motion | Best Thing About Video: Panthers, Rolls, Snakes, Gunz, and Boxing! This video has every fucking thing an awesome fucking video should have, LOL!!

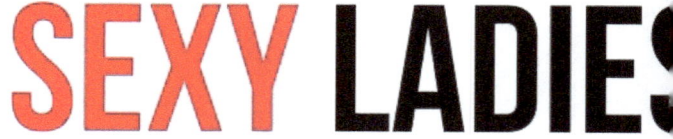

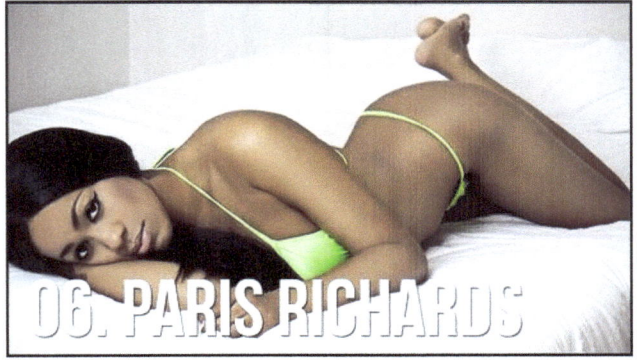

Instagram: Paris_richards | Music: Drake – The Language
Best Thing About Video: I LOVE BOOOBBBIIIEEESSS!!!

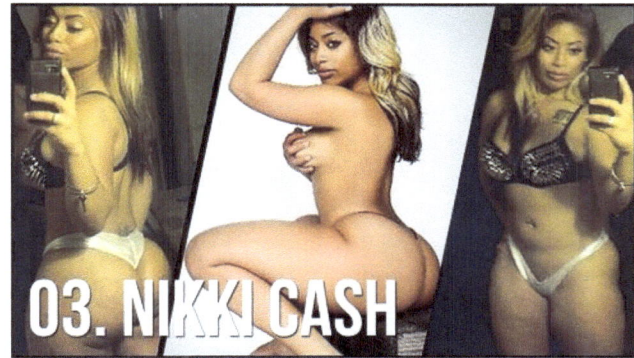

Instagram: Nikki_cash_ | Music: T-Pain feat B.o.B – Up Down | Best Thing About Video: Shawty got ass for daaayyysss!!!

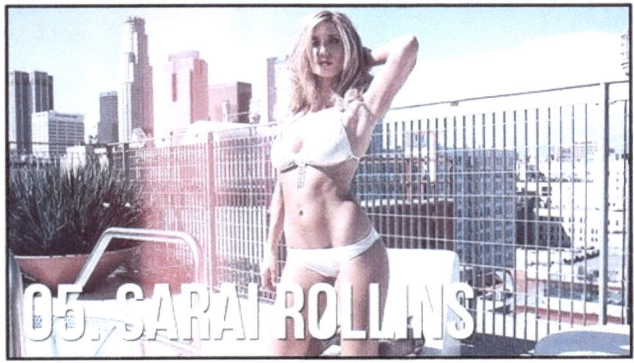

Instagram: Sarairollins | Music: Miguel – Girl With The Tattoo Remix | Directed By: Jahru | Best Thing About Video: A blonde with little pink nipples! This is quality in teasing!

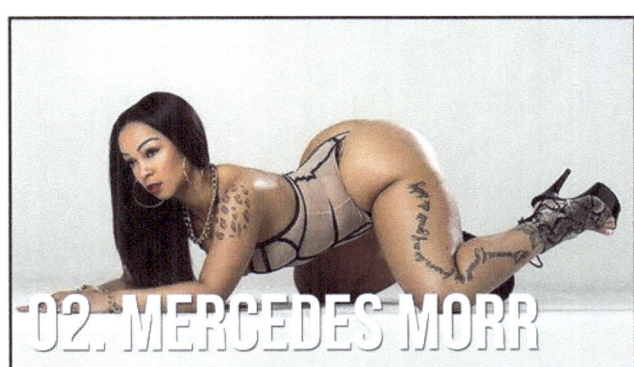

Instagram: missmercedesmorr | Directed By @jxnny5 | Best Thing About Video: I can tell you one thing, I'm strongly considering trading in my 325i!

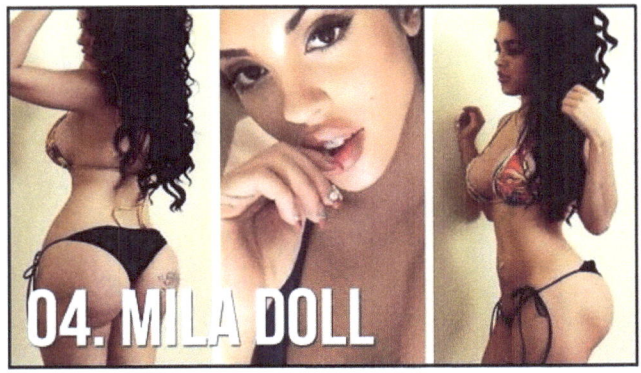

Instagram: miladoll323 | Music: Young Thug Feat. Nicki Minaj – Danny Glover | Directed By Jxnny5 | Best Thing About Video: Pretty Eyes! Pretty Smile! Full Frontal!

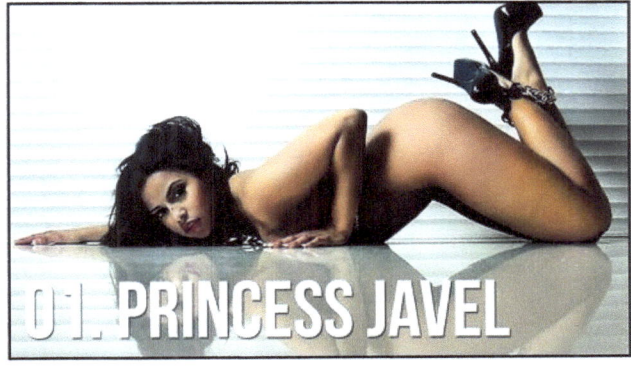

Instagram: Princessjavel | Music: The Weeknd – Live For (KLNV REMIX) | Directed By: Instagram.com/pierg1983 | Best Thing About Video: Gotta love that bounce. This shower scene is no punk! Peep the second half, you'll know it when you see it!

SEXY MUSIC! SEXY VIDEOS!

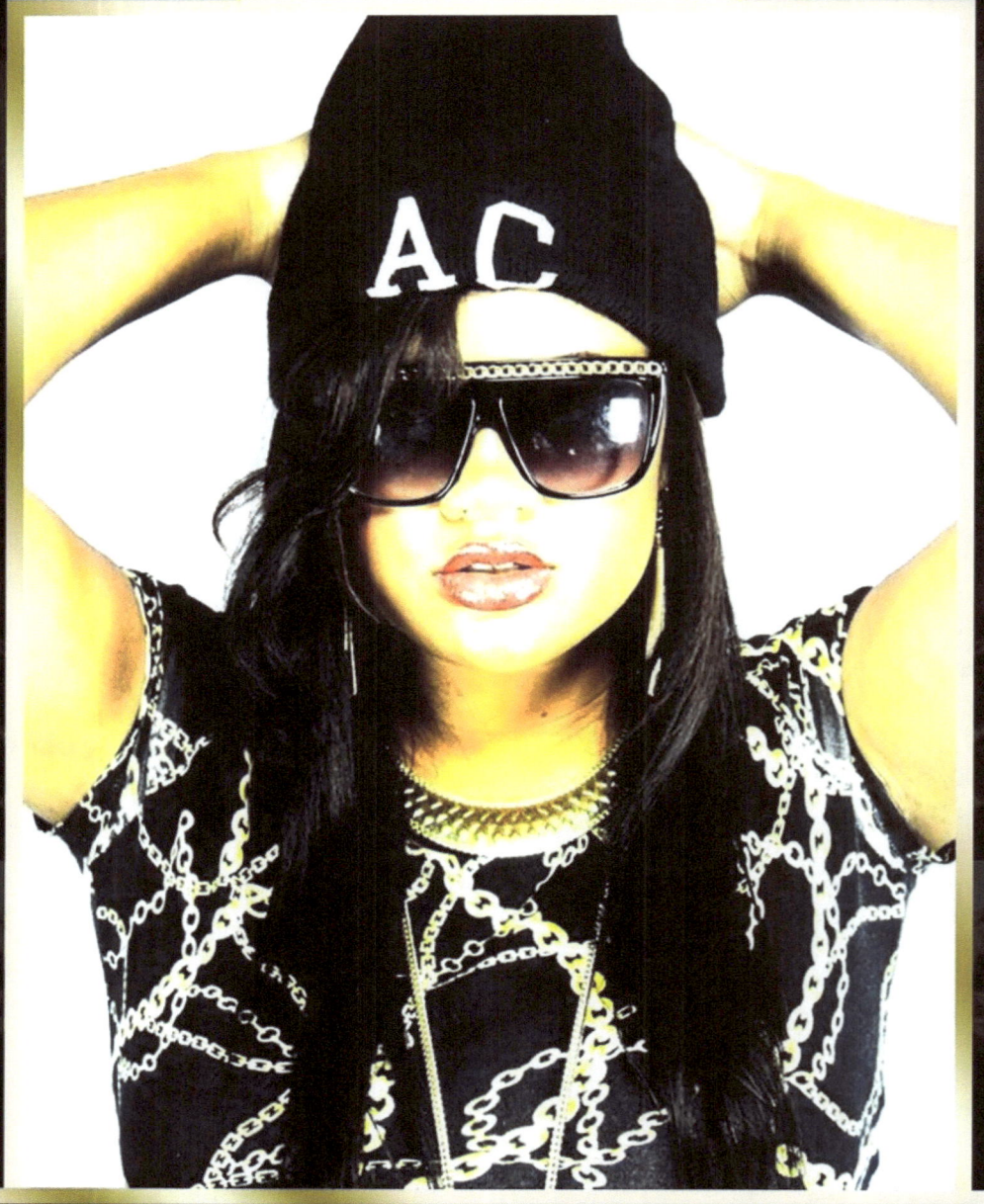

Ridin' Chi
ACSTYLE

WRITTEN BY: ERIKA JACKSON

RIDIN' CHI • ACSTYLE | FOXTAIL

Chicago has been the stomping ground of the most prominent figures in Hip Hop today; Common, Twista and Da Brat, just to name a few. There is a new millenial sweetheart of rap gearing to blow up the charts; AC Style. This ingenious, down to Earth young lady has a fierce dialect to her lyrics; while showing that she's more than just a pretty face.

FTM: AC Style, thank you so much for the opportunity to speak with you. How are you? You're a hard young lady to get in touch with.

AC: I'm good. Thank you; no problem. I've been so busy doing different things with my music and other projects I'm working on.

FTM: Cool; let's get to the music; how old were you when you started to listen to Hip Hop; who did you listen to growing up? Do you listen to other genres of music besides R & B and Hip Hop?

AC: I was ten maybe eleven; I listened to alot of Aaliyah, B2K...those were my favorites; I listened to some old school thanks to my parents; like Chaka Khan...being of Puerto Rican and Spanish decent, I love listening to Salsa...my parents raised me very well and to definitely appreciate all genres.

FTM: Now here is a pretty complex question; I don't want you to think that I believe your music sounds like everyone else; but what sets your music apart from other female MC's?

AC: Well...I actually sing too. So I'm not just a Hip Hop artist. My music is fun, laid back; focusing on having a good time. Like my new single; "Ridin" is just that; we're having a good time. Riding along Lake Shore Drive (which everyone loves to do; because of the view) we're looking good, we're in a nice ride; you know how it is...

FTM: Yes...one of my favorite strips of Chicago.

FTM: What do you think of the term "Chriaq"? Do you think it should be embraced? What do you think of Nicki Minaj's song "Chiraq"? Do you think she just tried to capitalize off the term at the expense of the people who live here?

AC: Well... I don't think people are really embracing it. It's just showing how the violence has really impacted our city. I don't even embrace it. I mean my snippet was just to show that people are fed up with the killings. As far as Nicki Minajs' version, I actually like it. I don't believe she was trying to market off the term; just shedding a light on the violence.

FTM: What was it like working with Shawnna? I know she's featured in your new single; but she's not in the video?

AC: She's a really cool person; gave me some really good advice about the industry; even stated that I was very talented. As far as the video, well she never showed up for the shoot for days...and finally we just had to do it without her.

FTM: Do you think it's better to be and independent artist or work with a major label?

AC: Well independent artists pretty much pay for everything themselves...promotion, production, etc...While if you're with a major label, they pay for your promotion, videos. I would rather be with a major label. Like I can't tell you the amount of money I've spent promoting myself....but it's been worth it. And actually I have a meeting with Atlantic Records in a few weeks. So in the meantime, I'm going to stack money...make some more moves and be more prepared to sign with the major label.

FTM: Congratulations on your meeting with Atlantic Records...that's huge!! Well as you know the ever influential Maya Angelou passed away this morning. Were you a fan?

AC: I was. Her poetry was beautiful. I love inspirational African American women.

FTM: Do you have any advice for the young women out there trying to make it in the industry?

AC: Yes! Never give up. Even though this is a male dominated industry, you can make it. Two years ago I wasn't able to picture where I am now. I worked hard, made alot of sacrifices. I have a huge fan base and I love what I do. I just want to be an inspiration for young ladies tolook up to.

FTM: Well....there you have it. You better believe you have not heard the last from AC Style. She is definitely a force to be reckoned with.

LOOK BOOK

SUMMER TIME
FRESHNESS

CROOKS & CASTLES
TRIUMPH SUNGLASSES
$90.00

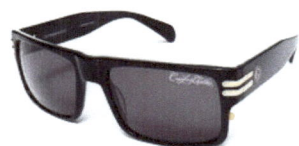

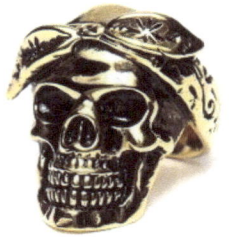

HAN CHOLO
CALI LOVE RING
$43.99

DNINE RESERVE
LIL B IMMACULATE FACE TEE
$138.00

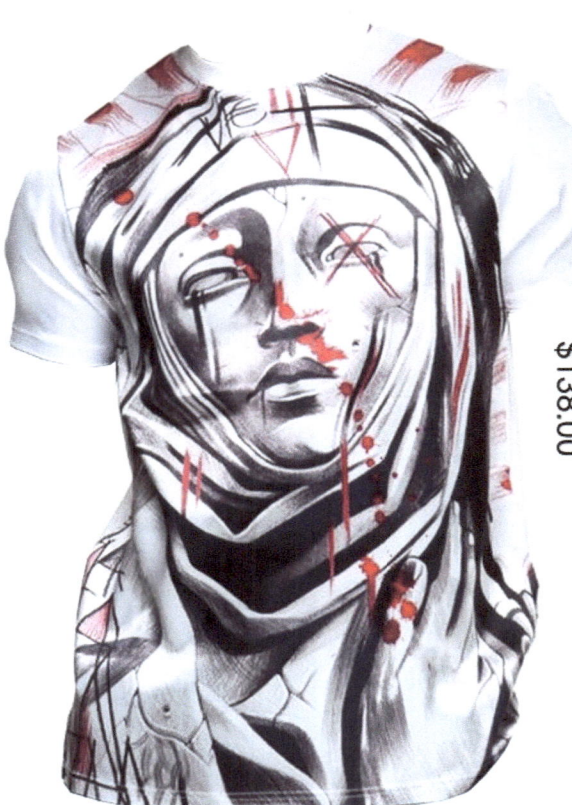

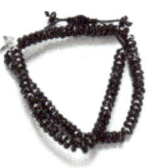

DJP OUTLET
TALON DOULBE WRAP METAL BEAD W/ LEATHER KNOT BRACELET
$70.00

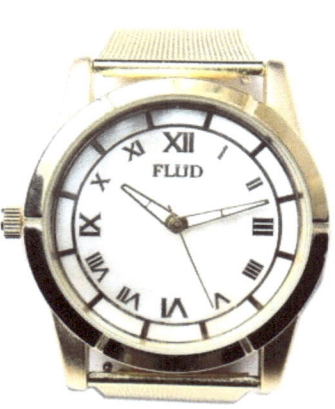

CROOKS & CASTLES
SUR CALIFAS BELT
$26.99

FLUD WATCHES
THE MOMENT WATCH
$72.00

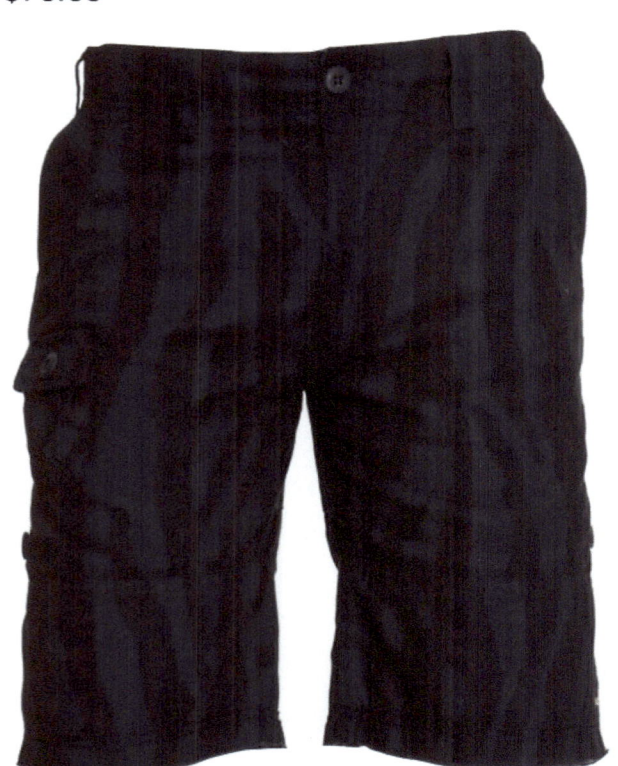

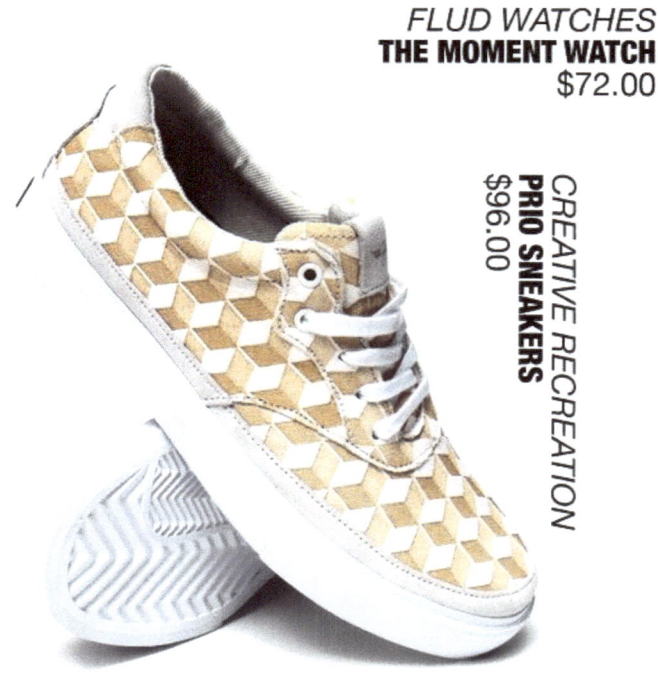

CREATIVE RECREATION
PRIO SNEAKERS
$96.00

DJP OUTLET
CONVERTIBLE BLACK ZEBRA PRINT FIELD TSHORT
$95.00

36 • FOXTAIL MAGAZINE

SHOE PORN

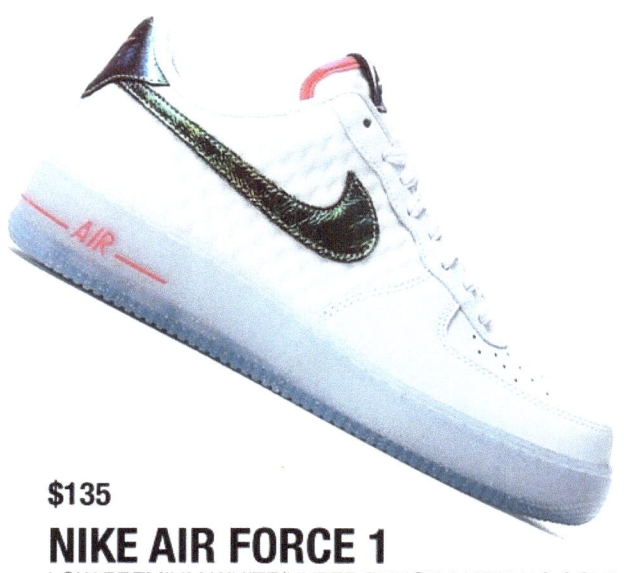

$135
NIKE AIR FORCE 1
LOW PREMIUM WHITE/HYPER PUNCH-METALLIC GOLD

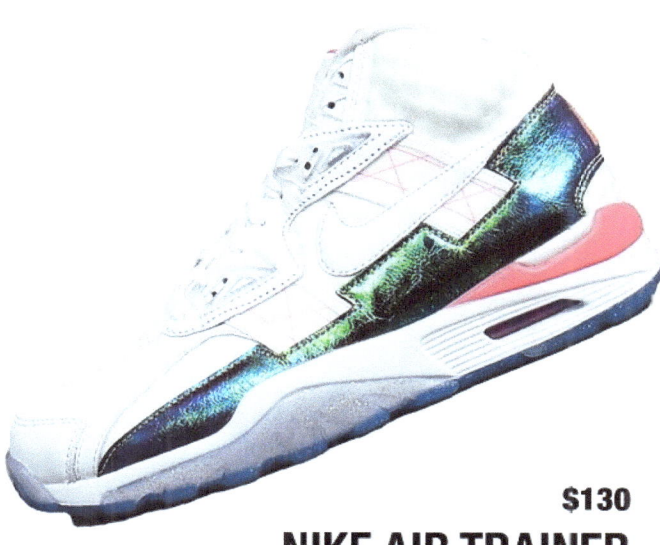

$130
NIKE AIR TRAINER
SC HIGH PREMIUM WHITE/HYPER PUNCH

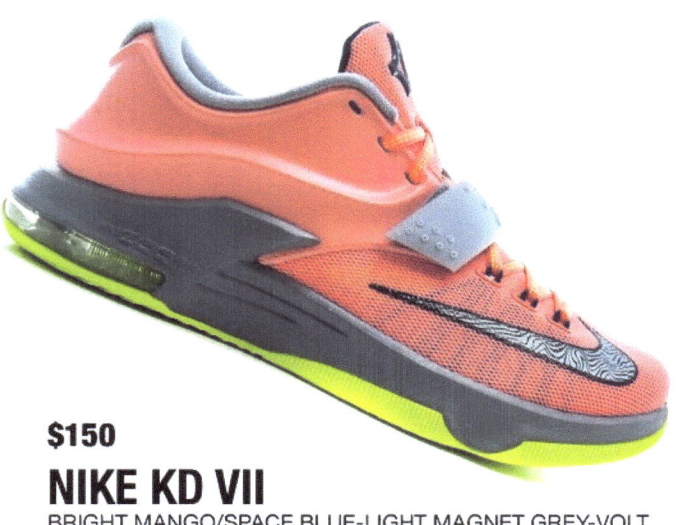

$150
NIKE KD VII
BRIGHT MANGO/SPACE BLUE-LIGHT MAGNET GREY-VOLT

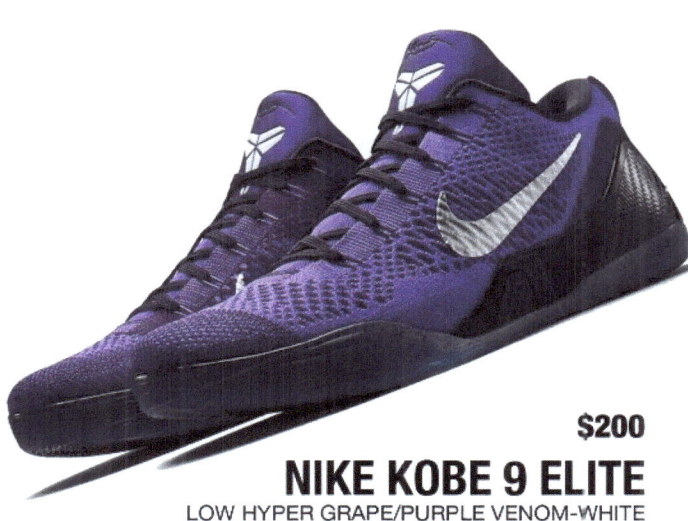

$200
NIKE KOBE 9 ELITE
LOW HYPER GRAPE/PURPLE VENOM-WHITE

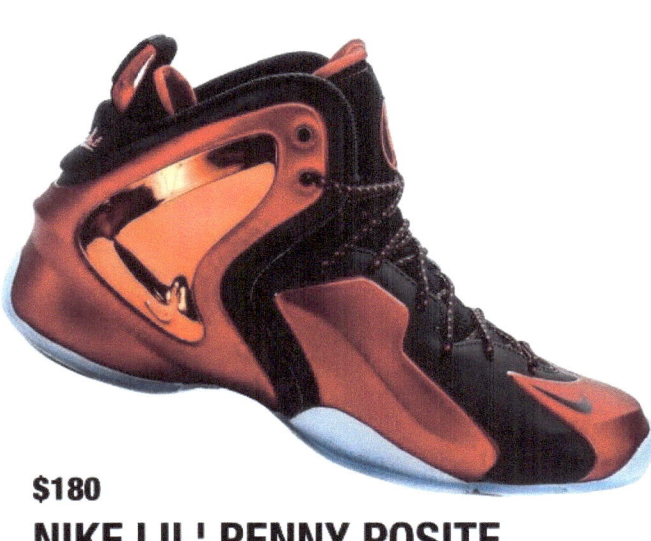

$180
NIKE LIL' PENNY POSITE
UNIVERSITY RED/BLACK-UNIVERSITY RED

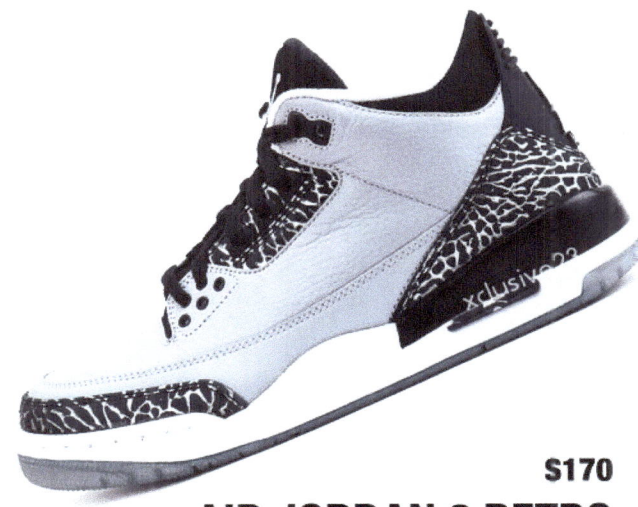

$170
AIR JORDAN 3 RETRO
WOLF GREY/METALLIC SILVER-BLACK-WHITE

CASIA JUSTINE

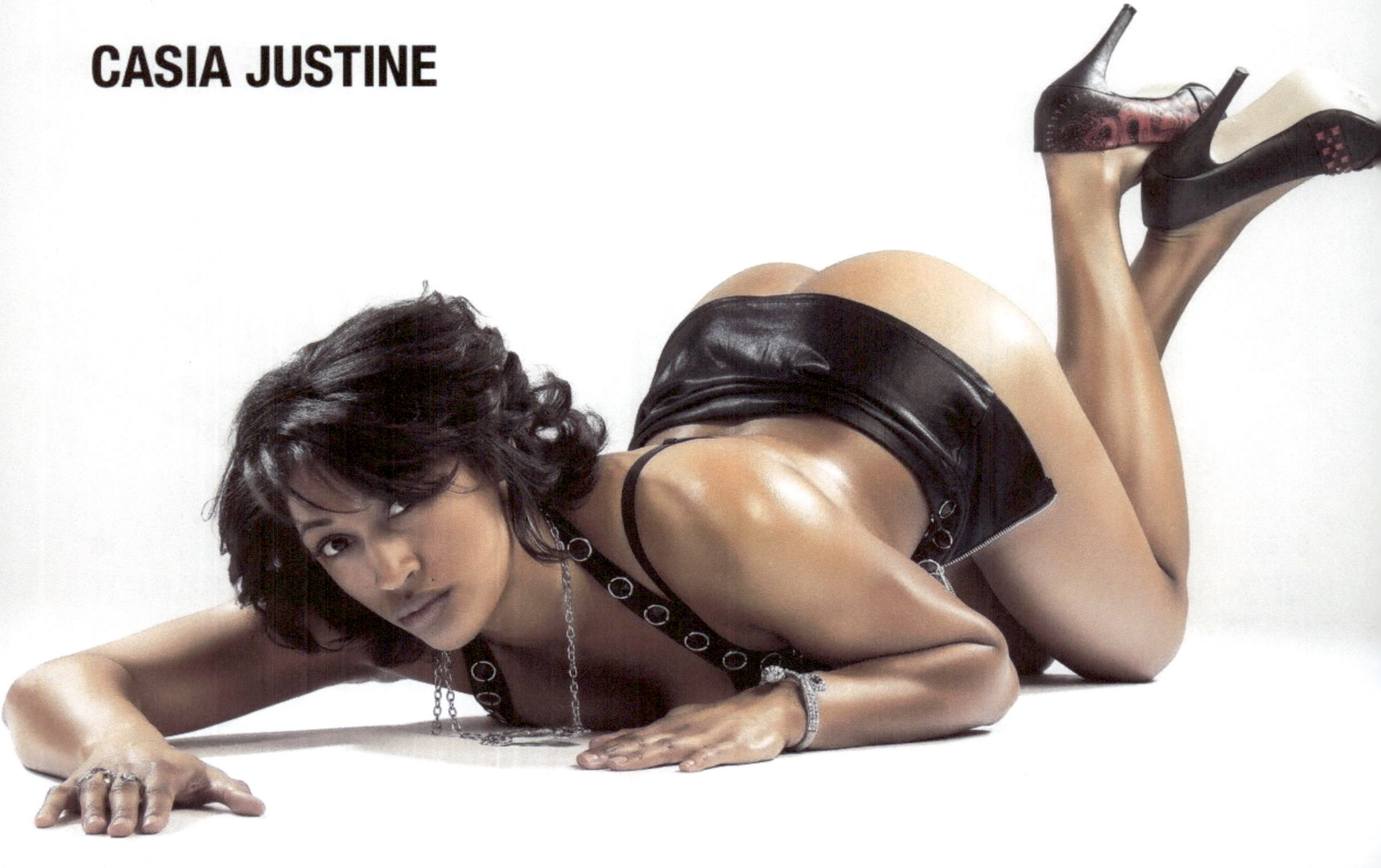

CASIA JUSTINE

PHOTOGRAPHY BY SINOVAH KANE

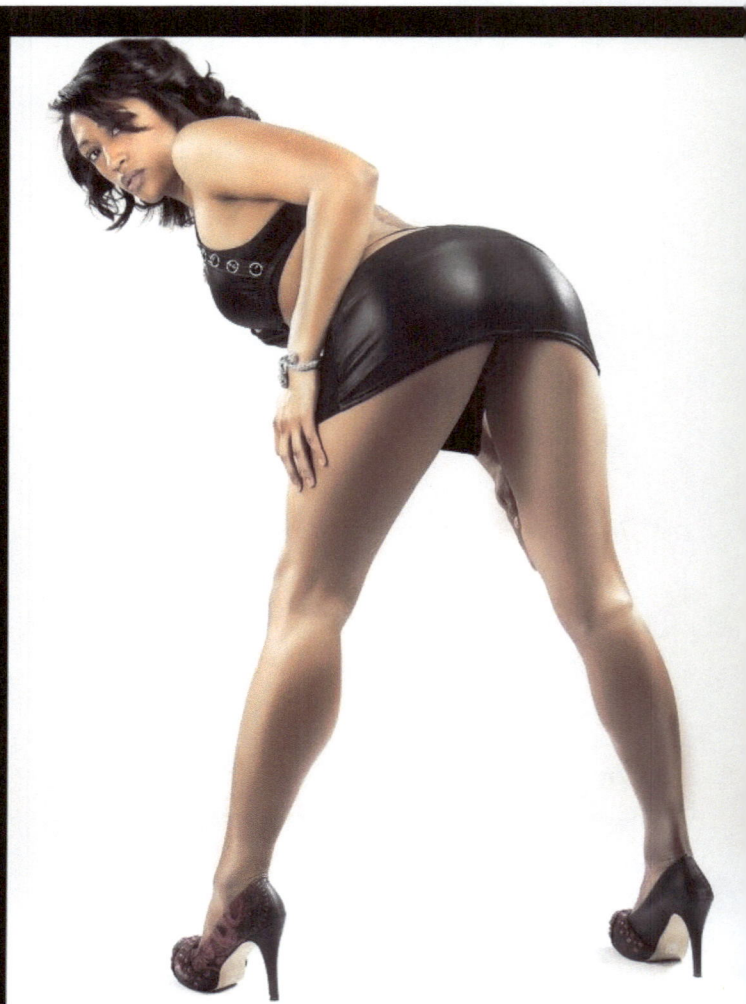

Age • *26* **Nationality** • *A mixed mocha chick with some Bahamian & American* **Place of Birth** • *Hollywood, CA* **Where Do You Rep** • *West Coast is the best coast!* **Profession** • *Health and Fitness Coach* **Relationship Status** • *Single* **Height** • *5'8"* **Weight** • *153* **Hair Color** • *Dark Brown* **Hair Length** • *Medium* **Eye Color** • *Dark Brown / Black*

CASIA JUSTINE
ALL ABOUT ME!

What's the worst lie you ever told? Did you get caught? *How about the worst truth?! I am pretty honest and I have told a guy that his breath smelled really bad and I refused to kiss him. I was as nice as I could be about his dragon breath.*

Would you rather be smart and ugly or dumb and beautiful? *Smart and ugly because plastic surgery can fix my face and body.*

If you could be invisible, where would you go and what would you do? *I would probably go where ever there are hot naked men and check them out, and the movies. I would never have to pay again.*

Do you consider yourself more of a "giver" or a "taker"? *I am definitely a giver, but I have my greedy days.*

What's your biggest turn on? *A guy that is honest and real. He knows how to communicate and not keep his true feelings to himself. I do not have time to be anyone's therapist, unless you want to pay me.*

What is the sexiest article of clothing you own? *Um, between crotch less panties and garter belts with thigh highs?? Who knows, I have a nice collection.*

What would the average person say about you? *I have a dirty mind which mostly stays in the gutter.*

What do guys compliment you most on? *My smile and eyes.*

Now, what would you like people to be attracted to? *That I lift weights and play with Kettlebells.*

What is your Fetish? *Going to sex shops to see what else I can add to my collection.*

If a guy doesn't have a lot of money, he'd better have... *great ideas for home activities where we do not have to spend money because I am not going to be the suga momma all the time!*

Have you ever had a one night stand? Details? *NOPE! I am actually a bit of a prude. I do 3-5 dates before I decided if you can handle me. I know what I like and I am not trying to train anyone in bed.*

CASIA JUSTINE

21 QUESTIONS CONT'D

13. If you had to sleep with a woman, who would be and how would you get her in bed? *I've been with women before, it's called "Hey, you ever been with a girl? Want to?" I would take Rihanna though.*

14. What do you normally sleep in? *No joke, a muumuu right now! I am single, so I have no one to impress at the moment.*

15. What would you consider your strongest attribute? *I am a genuine person. Plain and simple.*

16. What do you like best about being a model? *I get to see how I've progressed over the years and I get to be a muse. Plus I've met some really awesome photographers, makeup artists, and other models throughout the years.*

17. Do you own any adult videos? *Yes! I use to work for Hustler in West Hollywood and Chicago. I was with the company for almost 3 years and they helped increase my collection of adult fun!*

18. If you were a waiter and a customer was being rude, would you spit in their food? *Gross, no! That is absolutely foul and disgusting. Depending on how rude they were being, I would call them out on their bull crap. I can always get another job.*

19. What's the difference between sex and making love? *Making love means you would have a deeper connection with that person and it also involves more kissing and looking into each other's eyes.*

20. Do you have any secret weaknesses or guilty pleasures? *Yes, I LOVE playing air hockey and video games. I am also a sucker for men with great bodies!*

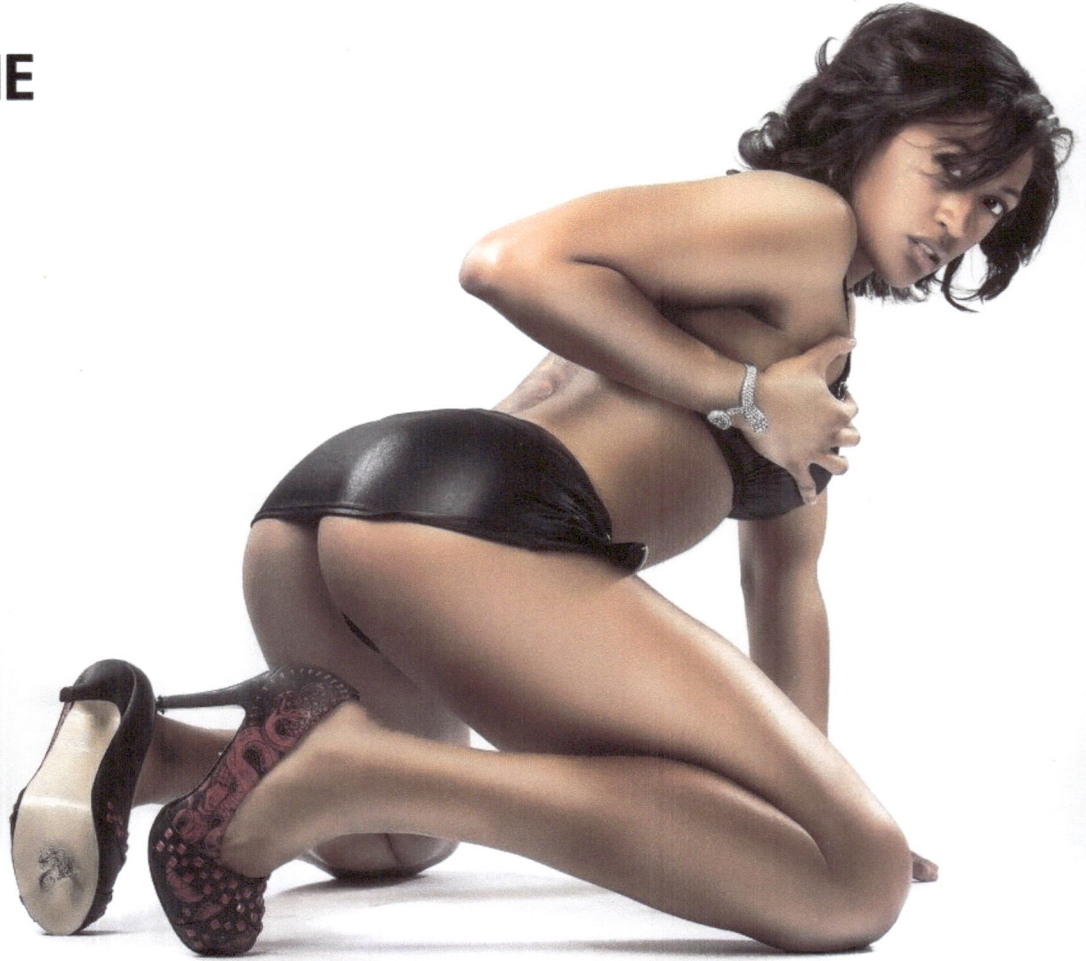

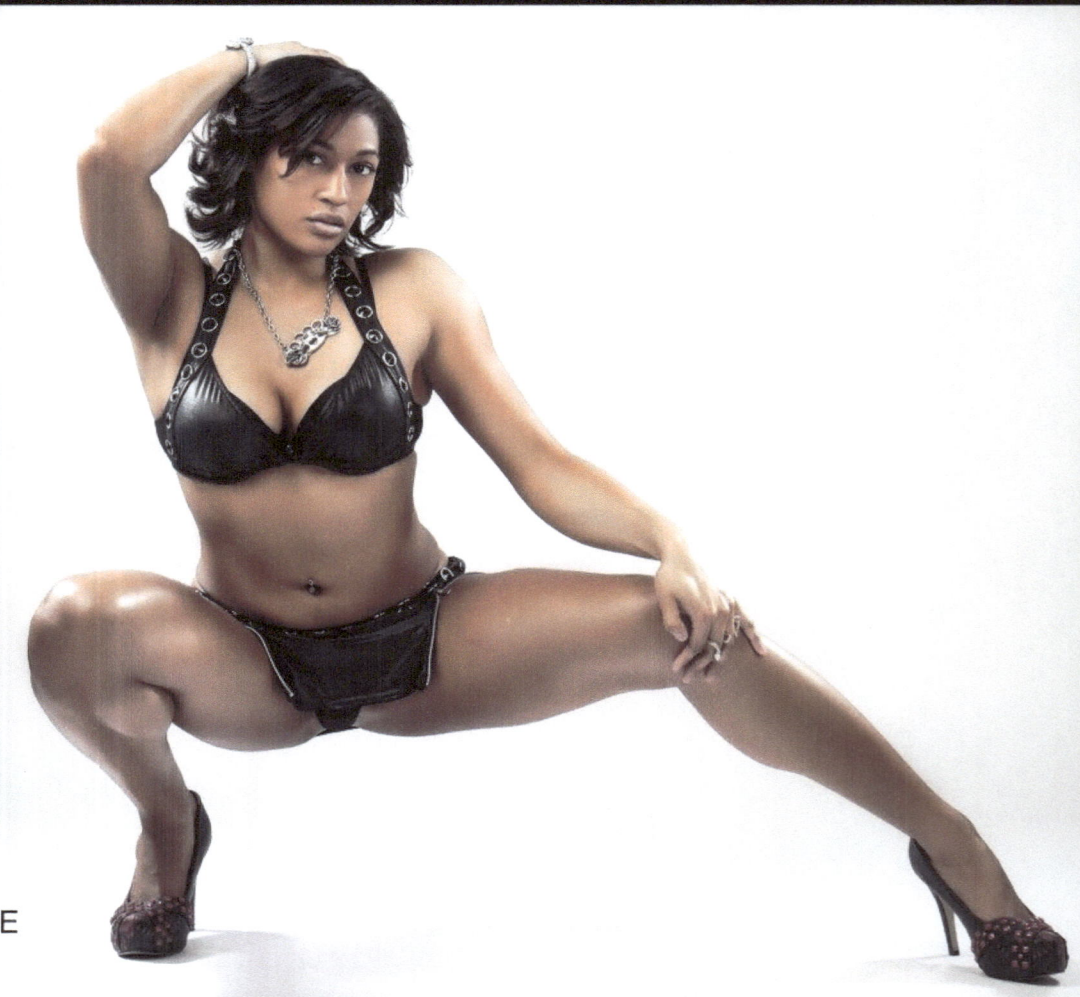

40 • FOXTAIL MAGAZINE

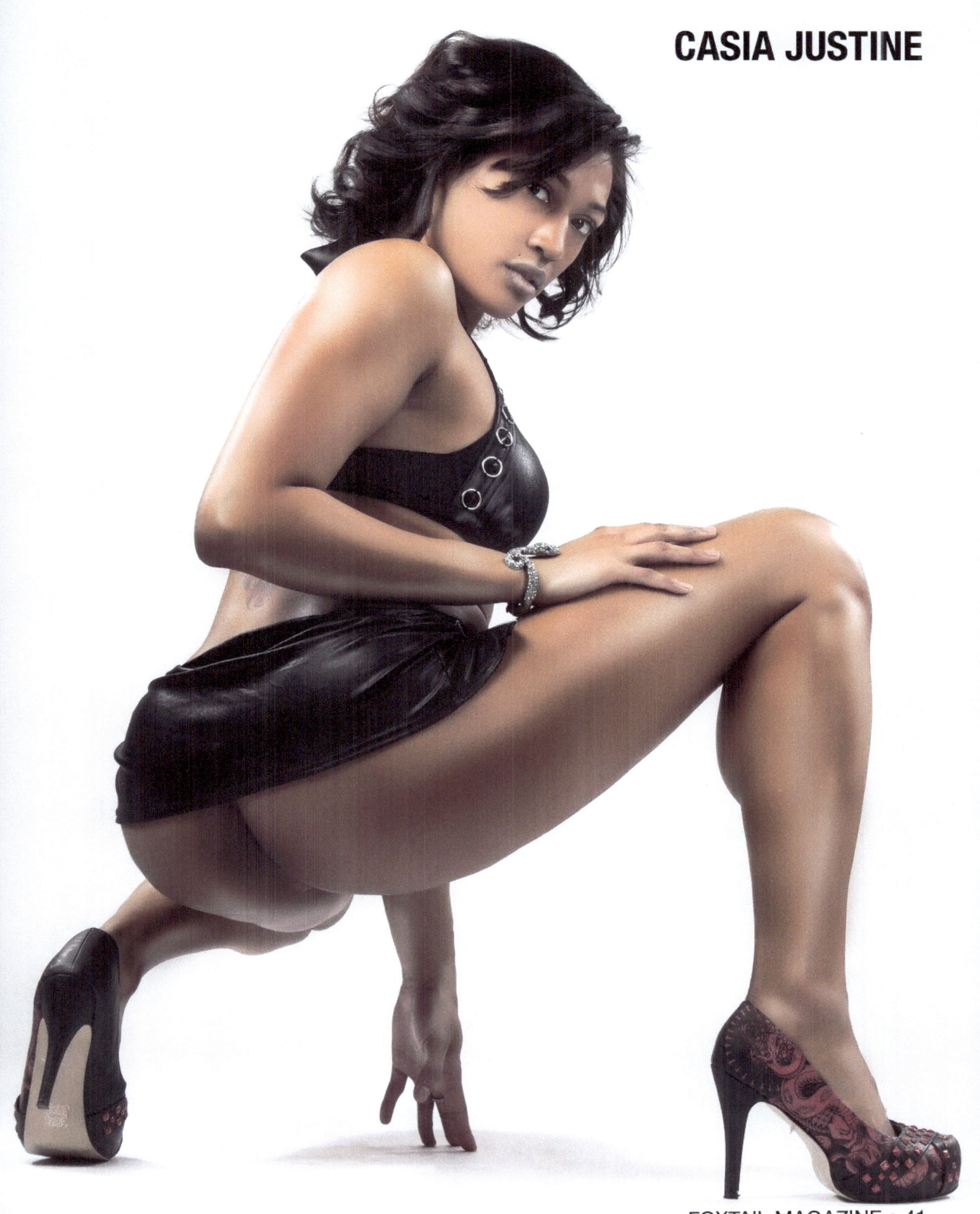

PUT DOWN YOUR

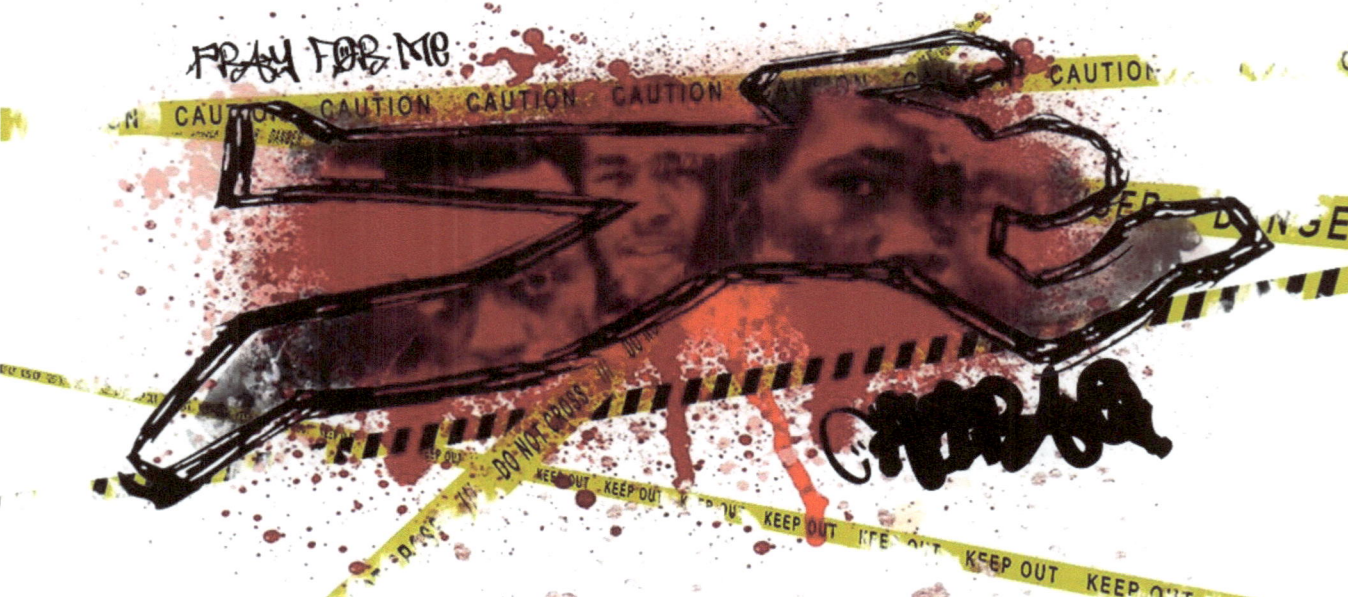

GUNS CHICAGO

FOXTAIL MAGAZINE

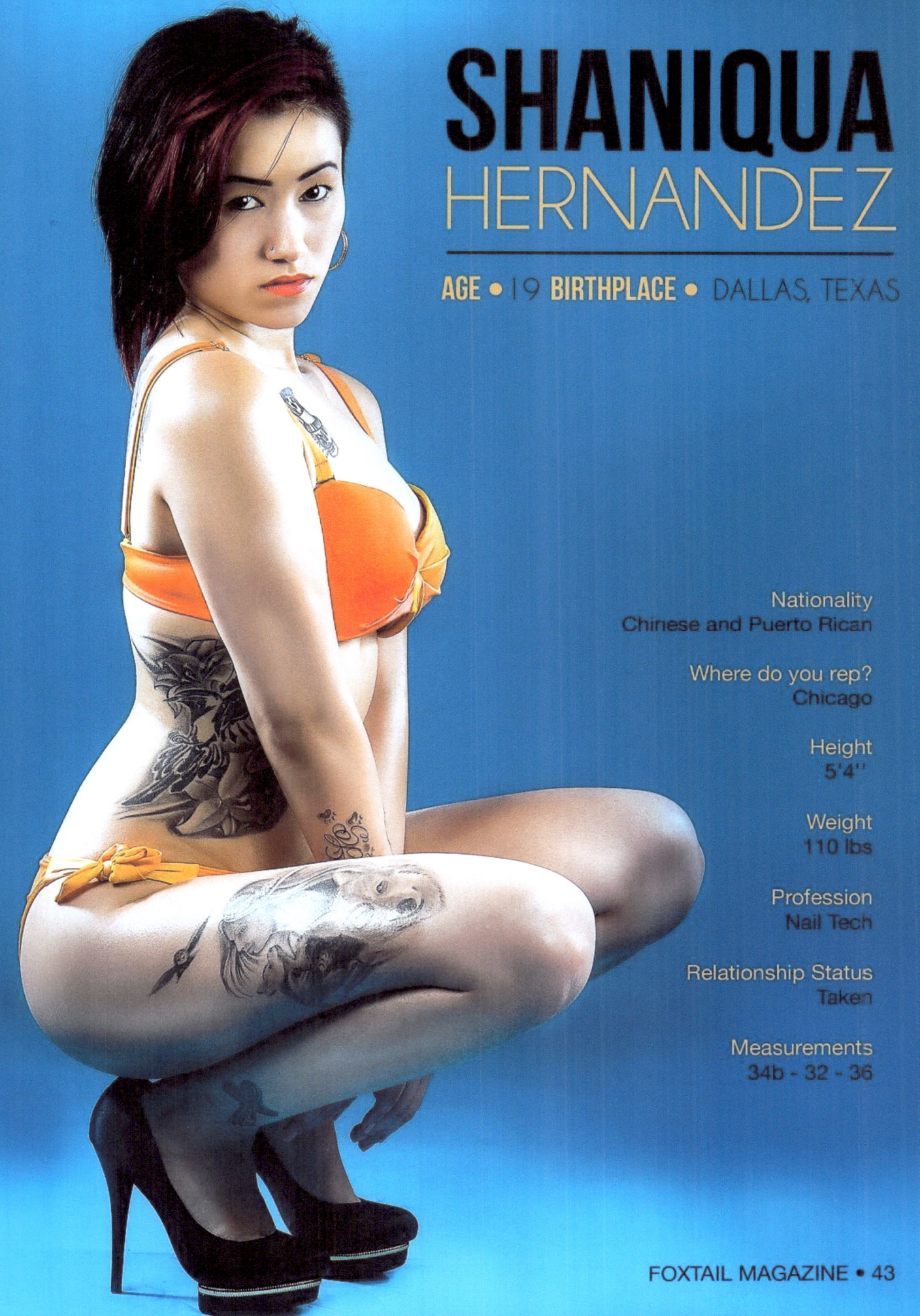

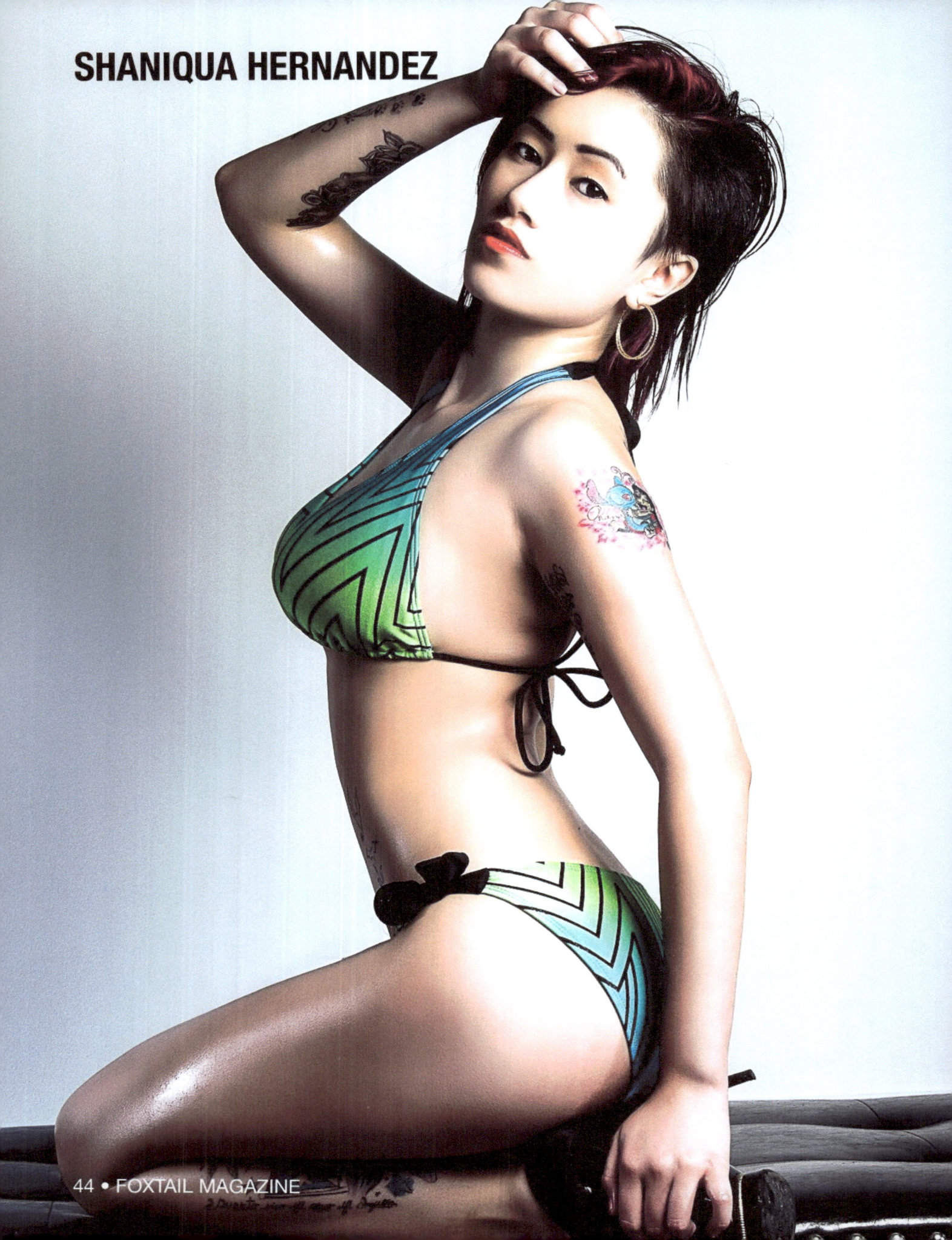

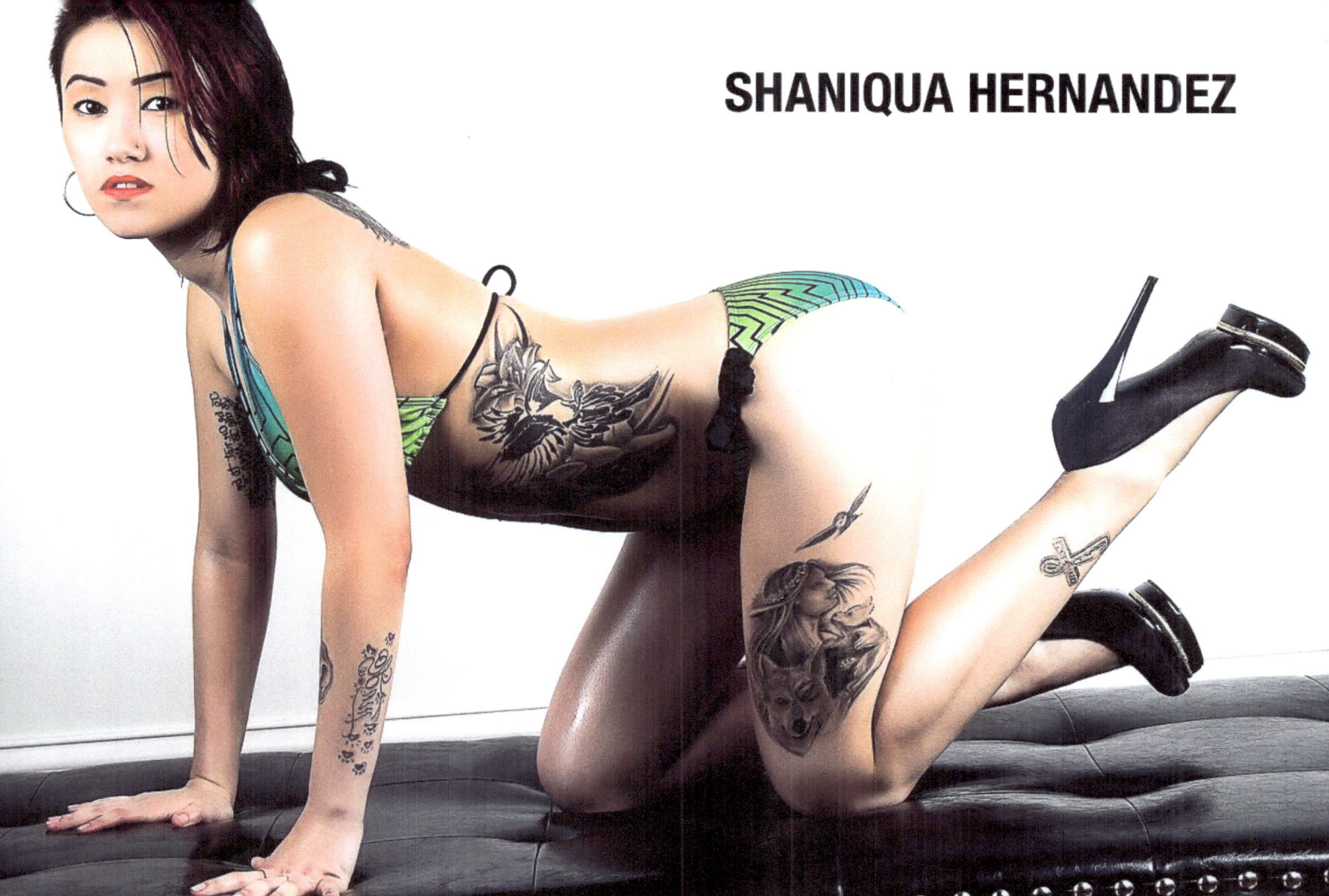

SHANIQUA HERNANDEZ

ALL ABOUT ME!

What's the worst lie you ever told? Did you get caught? *I was suppose to go hang out with my girlfriends, but instead I decided to hang out at my boyfriend's house for a little late night fun. I had a great time and, no, I never got caught!*

Would you rather be smart and ugly or dumb and beautiful? *I can't choose between either because I am both smart and beautiful, so I'm like the prefect balance.*

If you could be invisible, where would you go and what would you do? *It's probably a little cliche, but hey, I'm invisible. If I was invincible, I hit the bank and take all the money.*

Do you consider yourself more of a "giver" or a "taker"? *I would definitely consider myself a giver. Just don't take to much, or you'll regret it.*

What's your biggest turn on? *The best thing you can do to get me going is by placing little small kisses on my neck.*

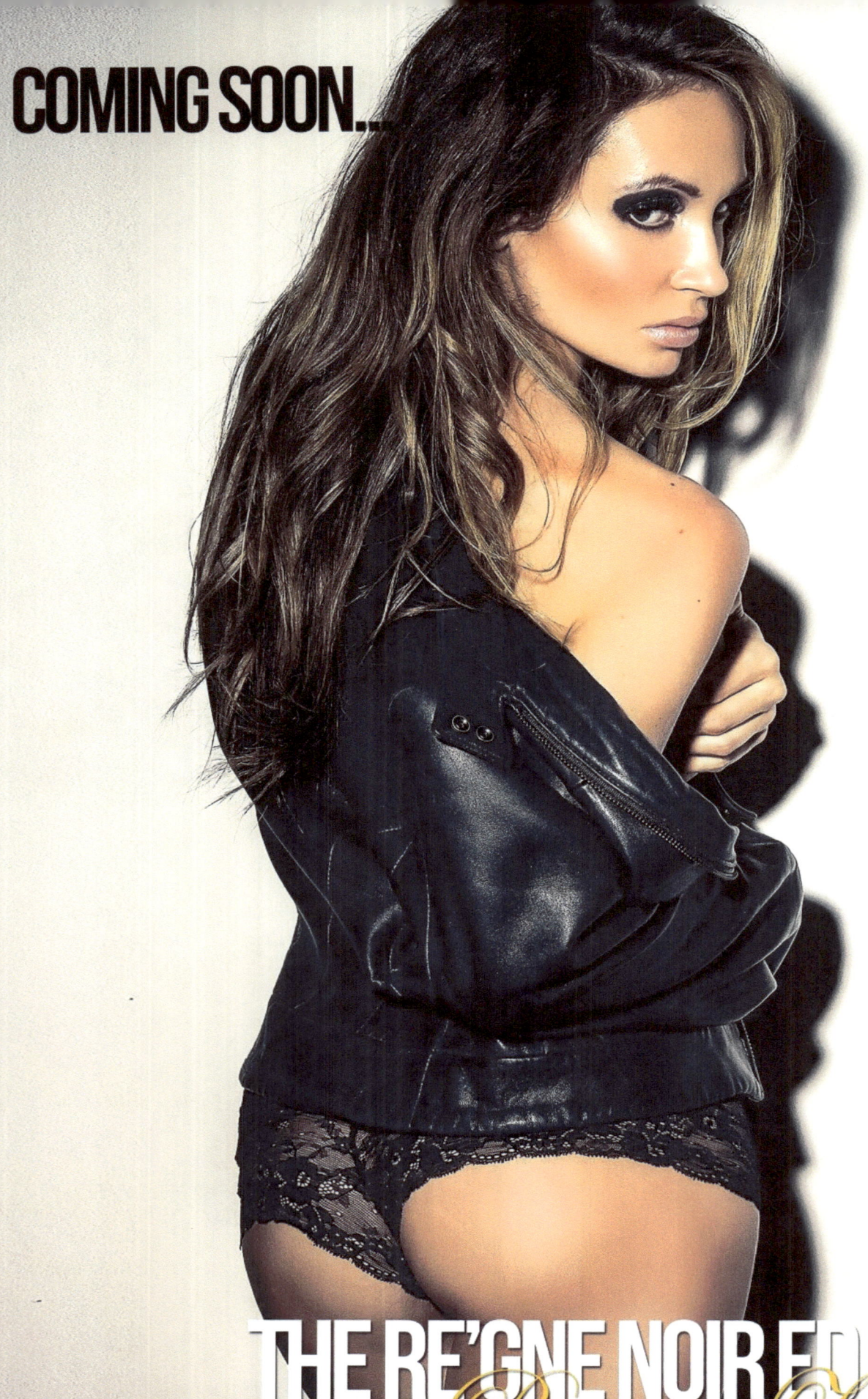

GET **FOXTAIL** MAGAZINE
On the Devices that Matter to You the Most!!!

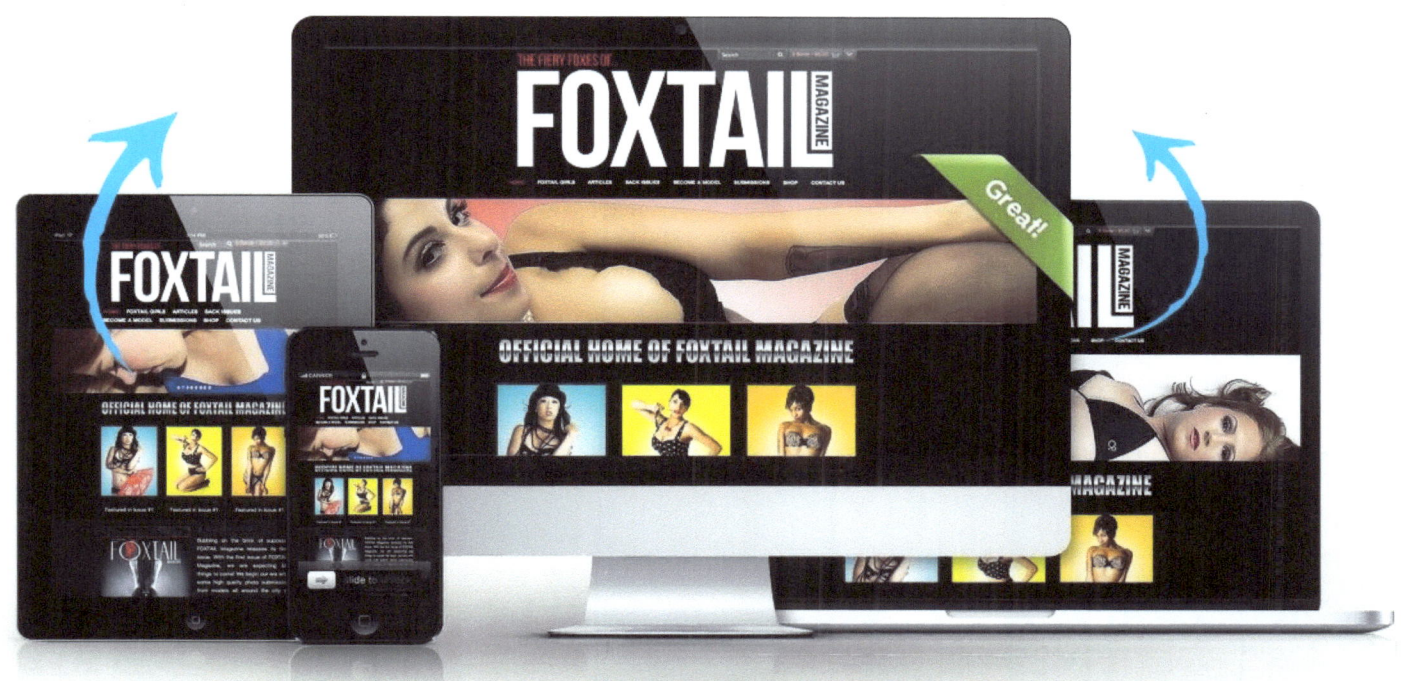

ADVERTISE
WITH
FOXTAIL MAGAZINE

FOR MORE INFOMATION, SEND EMAIL TO: ADVERTISING@FOXTAILMAG.COM

www.ingramcontent.com/pod-product-compliance
Lightning Source LLC
Chambersburg PA
CBHW051223220526
45473CB00003B/1148